PRACTICAL PROJECTS TO MAKE
40 BIRD BOXES
FEEDERS AND BIRDBATHS

PRACTICAL PROJECTS TO MAKE
40 BIRD BOXES
FEEDERS AND BIRDBATHS

ATTRACT BIRDS TO YOUR GARDEN BY CREATING NEST BOXES, ROOSTS,
BIRDHOUSES, DOVECOTES, TABLES, FEEDING STATIONS AND BIRDBATHS

CONTRIBUTING EDITOR: JEN GREEN

HERMES
HOUSE

This edition is published by Hermes House,
an imprint of Anness Publishing Ltd,
Blaby Road, Wigston, Leicestershire LE18 4SE
info@anness.com

www.hermeshouse.com; www.annesspublishing.com

If you like the images in this book and would like to investigate using them for publishing, promotions or advertising, please visit our website www.practicalpictures.com for more information.

Publisher: Joanna Lorenz
Senior Editor: Felicity Forster
Text: Dr Jen Green, Deena Beverley, Mary Maguire
    and Andrew Newton-Cox
Photography: David Parmiter and Peter Williams
Designer: Nigel Partridge
Production Controller: Christine Ni

ETHICAL TRADING POLICY
At Anness Publishing we believe that business should be conducted in an ethical and ecologically sustainable way, with respect for the environment and a proper regard to the replacement of the natural resources we employ.

As a publisher, we use a lot of wood pulp to make high-quality paper for printing, and that wood commonly comes from spruce trees. We are therefore currently growing more than 750,000 trees in three Scottish forest plantations: Berrymoss (130 hectares/320 acres), West Touxhill (125 hectares/305 acres) and Deveron Forest (75 hectares/185 acres). The forests we manage contain more than 3.5 times the number of trees employed each year in making paper for the books we manufacture.

Because of this ongoing ecological investment programme, you, as our customer, can have the pleasure and reassurance of knowing that a tree is being cultivated on your behalf to naturally replace the materials used to make the book you are holding.

Our forestry programme is run in accordance with the UK Woodland Assurance Scheme (UKWAS) and will be certified by the internationally recognized Forest Stewardship Council (FSC). The FSC is a non-government organization dedicated to promoting responsible management of the world's forests. Certification ensures forests are managed in an environmentally sustainable and socially responsible way. For further information about this scheme, go to www.annesspublishing.com/trees.

A CIP catalogue record for this book is available from the British Library.

Previously published as part of a larger volume, *An Illustrated Practical Guide to Attracting and Feeding Garden Birds*

PUBLISHER'S NOTE
Although the advice and information in this book are believed to be accurate and true at the time of going to press, neither the authors nor the publisher can accept any legal responsibility or liability for any errors or omissions that may have been made nor for any inaccuracies nor for any loss, harm or injury that comes about from following instructions or advice in this book.

CONTENTS

INTRODUCTION

Birds have been a source of fascination and inspiration to people for many years. Attracting birds to your garden and observing the variety of species that visit can develop into an exciting and absorbing pastime – and one which offers an unparalleled insight into the natural world.

Whether your garden or backyard is in the countryside, a town or a city, it can play an important part in the conservation of wildlife, and especially birds. As farming becomes more intensive, and more and more of the countryside is swallowed up by new housing and industrial developments, the natural habitats of many birds are being reduced or lost altogether. Gardens are now more essential for the survival of birds than ever. A little planning will ensure that your garden is a welcoming haven for birds.

HELPING BIRDS

The average garden is regularly visited by 15–20 species of birds, with occasional visits from 10 less common species. By simply erecting a bird table, nest box and birdbath, you will not only be offering nature a helping hand, you will also provide yourself with hours of interest

Below: *Birds will come flocking to your garden if you provide them with a wide range of seeds, nuts and dried fruit.*

and entertainment. Your helpful garden friends will return the favour by controlling pests, such as aphids, slugs and snails, that threaten your flower-beds and vegetable patch.

ABOUT THIS BOOK

This book is a celebration of garden birds and how to attract and support them by making hanging feeders, bird tables, birdbaths, nesting materials dispensers, nest boxes and dovecotes. A charming addition to any garden, these structures help to ornament and personalize it, and give an even greater satisfaction if you have made them yourself.

The book offers a wide range of projects that will encourage birds, ranging from simple decorated nest boxes to highly elaborate birdhouses. There are creative ideas for feeders and birdbaths, with something to suit every garden and every level of practical expertise. There are also tips on maintaining birdhouses, where and when to site them, and how to keep visiting

Above: *Once you have discovered ways of enticing birds into your garden, you might be rewarded with sights such as this.*

birds safe from predators. All the projects in the book represent practical as well as attractive solutions for providing food, drink and shelter for birds.

There are templates at the back of the book to help you construct the more complex projects, as well as tables of dimensions that give measurements for the floor sizes, box depths, heights and hole diameters to suit a range of different bird species.

Creating a haven for garden birds is a thoroughly satisfying activity. It is pure joy when you see a bird starting to build its new home in a nest box that you have made yourself. The whole experience is rewarding, from the pleasure of watching parent birds carrying food to the young in the nest, to the wait for fledglings to emerge and finally take wing.

Right: *Hanging bird feeders are very attractive and provide the opportunity to observe birds' acrobatic abilities.*

ATTRACTING BIRDS TO YOUR GARDEN

Birds are a delight in the garden at all times of year. In spring and summer their singing provides pleasure, while in winter their colourful plumage helps to brighten dull days. Urban gardens can be havens for wild birds, especially if you put out food and water. Birds will soon come to know it as a food source, and it will become a regular stopping-off point. If nest boxes are provided, birds may well set up home too. There is immense satisfaction to be had from knowing that you are helping wild bird populations to thrive and from watching the species that come to feed.

Left: *In spring, the provision of foods and also nesting materials may help many types of birds to rear their young successfully.*

Above: *Feeders containing different foods placed at varying heights in the garden will help to attract a greater variety of birds.*

Above: *House sparrows are among the bird species that benefit from the provision of seeds and nuts in feeders.*

Above: *Swallows usually build mud nests under the eaves of houses. This adult has been induced to nest in a whimsical box.*

STRUCTURES TO ATTRACT BIRDS

By providing a range of feeding, nesting and watering structures and distributing them around the garden, you can attract a wide range of bird species. Tables, feeders, nest boxes, birdhouses, roosts and birdbaths are also beautiful structures in their own right, and will enhance any garden.

Seeing birds regularly visiting your garden is enormously rewarding, and the inclusion of a few simple structures will ensure that your garden is attractive to birds.

BIRD TABLES

A bird table is the most obvious and effortless way to attract birds into your garden, and winter is the best time to set one up, when the natural food supply is scarce and the ground too hard for the birds to penetrate with their beaks.

Your bird table may be supported on a post or brackets or it may hang from a branch. It needs a roof to keep the rain off and a rim to prevent the food from being blown away. Other additions, such as a scrap basket, seed tube or water port, may be incorporated into the design.

FEEDERS

Pet and garden suppliers stock a huge range of feeders for different types of nuts or seeds. These are useful, as seeds are otherwise easily scattered and blown away. Some of the designs that are readily available are squirrel-proof. Mesh feeders are designed to dispense nuts, while feeders made of plastic tubing are designed for seeds.

There are also feeders that are designed to be stuck on to a window. Provided you don't mind the birds making a mess of your window and walls, these will enable you to study your avian visitors at close proximity. As an alternative to buying feeders, you could try making your own, using the ideas for constructing inexpensive versions given later in this book.

NEST BOXES

Simple nest boxes are generally designed to hang from a tree or wall. Ready-crafted boxes may be made of plain wood, preserved with creosote, or rustic-looking hollowed-out logs fitted with roofs. It is often best to choose a box that is designed with a specific type of bird in mind. The all-important factor is the size of the entry hole to admit nesting birds.

If you are building your own nest box, wood is probably the best material to use, though if it is thinner than 15mm (⅝in) it may warp and won't offer much insulation. Old floorboards are a good source of timber if you can get them, as they are well seasoned. Although softwood is easier to work with, hardwoods such as oak are longer lasting. Exterior or marine plywood can be used in any situation.

Wherever possible, use the wood with the grain running vertically. This will help the rain to drain off. Glue all joints before screwing them together, or use galvanized nails, which are better for damp conditions as they will not rust easily.

The most important thing is that the box should be warm and dry, but not so airtight that condensation becomes a problem. Some birdhouse-builders drill small holes high on the sides of the box to create ventilation and so lessen condensation. There is still plenty of room for improvement with traditional designs and materials, so feel free to experiment.

BIRDHOUSES

These are ornamental versions of nest boxes. They have a dual purpose, providing a safe nesting site for birds while also satisfying your aesthetic need to decorate the garden. Designs ranging from plain to highly ornamental are available from bird reserves, garden and pet shops, and are usually post-mounted. The important thing to check when buying a birdhouse is that

Left: *Many types of roofed bird tables can be purchased quite cheaply. Better still, you can construct your own.*

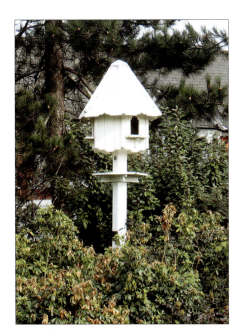

Above: *A post-mounted dovecote provides a sheltering place for pigeons, and also makes an attractive addition to the garden. Choose a site that is protected from prevailing winds, rain and too much sun.*

Above: *Birds need regular bathing to keep their feathers in good condition. To ensure a good wetting, they often dip down and use their wings and tail to splash the water.*

it will fulfil the requirements of the type of birds you want to attract. Each of the projects featured here indicates the typical inhabitants that it is designed for, although you also need to consider local breeds.

ROOSTS

Most birds sleep at night, with their beaks hidden under one shoulder, their heads tucked in and their feathers puffed up to keep them warm. They need regular roosting places that are protected from the elements and from predators. Birds will often use nest boxes for this purpose, so don't despair if your house or box has not been selected for a nest site – it is still probably being used as a roost or shelter, so it will be doing an important job, and possibly saving birds' lives in severe weather conditions, including icy temperatures and storms.

BIRDBATHS

Birds get most of the water that they require from their food, but they still need supplies to supplement this. Seed-eaters, for example, need plenty of drinking water

Right: *These cosy woven roosts provide a place for birds to sleep or shelter from inclement weather. They are inexpensive and look the part tucked between the branches of a tree.*

to compensate for the lack of moisture in their diet. Most birds drink by dipping their beaks into the water, then tilting their heads back, though pigeons are able to suck water up through their bills. Because birds don't sweat, they need another way to keep cool: they lose moisture by opening their mouths and panting.

The main purpose of providing water for birds is not for drinking but for bathing. They need to keep their feathers in good condition for both flight and insulation, and baths are just as important in winter as they are in summer. If their plumage is not

properly maintained they will not survive the cold winter nights. So in frosty weather, it is vital to check daily that your birdbath has not frozen over.

You will find that a design for a birdbath with an ingenious anti-freezing device has been included in this book. It is important never to put antifreeze or salt into the water, as this can kill birds.

FEEDING BIRDS

The simplest way to attract birds to your garden, or even window box, is to put out food for them, particularly during the months of winter when natural foods become much scarcer. However, you may provide appropriate food for garden birds throughout the year if you wish.

Whatever feeding method you decide upon, be consistent. A wasted journey to an empty bird table uses a bird's precious energy supply, especially as winter progresses and food becomes more difficult to find. Ideally, feed birds twice a day in winter: once in the early morning and again in the early afternoon.

In spring and summer, feeding can still be helpful, but do follow rules for safety and hygiene. Do not use peanuts unless they are in a mesh container; this will prevent the larger pieces, which can choke baby birds, from being removed. In summer, avoid fat cakes; the fat will melt and become very messy, and can also glue birds' beaks together.

Below: *Roofed bird tables will keep birds – and the food provided – dry in wet weather. This one was made from pieces of fallen wood collected from the forest floor.*

Above: *Lard cakes studded with seeds appeal to many varieties of bird, including this starling (*Sturnus vulgaris*).*

Above: *Ground feeders provide food for birds that forage for seeds at ground level, such as dunnocks, finches and thrushes.*

BIRD TABLES

Ideally, a bird table should be placed approximately 2–3m (6½–10ft) from a bush or tree, which can provide safety for birds in case of danger, and at least 5m (16½ft) from the house. Many birds are nervous of open sites, but equally they can have accidents flying into house windows, and may be scared away by the movement of people inside the house. Window stickers featuring birds of prey are available which, when stuck to the window panes, indicate the presence of an otherwise invisible surface and will deter smaller birds from flying too close to the house.

A bird table gives you a clear view of feeding birds, and offers the birds some protection against predators and the elements. Use wood that has not been treated with wood preservative if you are making your own table. A roof will keep the food and the birds dry. If you don't make a roof, drill a few holes in the floor of the table for drainage. A small lip around the edge of the food table can prevent lighter food items from being blown away by wind. The bird table must be cleaned from time to

Above: *A wire mesh around the food source prevents the birds from extracting whole peanuts. This is important during the nesting season because young nestlings and fledglings can choke on whole nuts.*

time and any food that is past its best should be removed. An adequate supply of water should be provided all year round, but this can be as simple as a bowl of water placed on the surface of the table, or a separate facility.

GROUND STATIONS

Some birds, such as dunnocks, song thrushes and American robins, are habitual ground feeders. Pheasants, finches, buntings and turtle doves may also be attracted to ground feeding stations – a wooden or plastic hopper secured to a strong base. Place a ground feeder away from the bird table, so that the food is not contaminated by droppings from the birds above.

HANGING FEEDERS

Some species, such as tits, titmice and chickadees, that are adapted to feeding in trees will benefit from a more challenging feeder. These birds can cling upside-down from various types of hanging feeders, and may be joined by siskins and nuthatches. Many types of feeder are available, or you can make or adapt your own, using the

Above: *Seed balls and strings of nuts are a welcome supplement to the meagre diet which is available to many birds in winter. Remember to keep a supply of fresh water on hand, as dried food does not contain enough natural moisture.*

projects in this book. Some foods are also suitable for hanging without a feeder, for example, peanuts in their shells, half coconuts, popcorn garlands and also fat cakes on strings.

Right: *Hanging feeders offer an easy challenge to species with natural acrobatic abilities, such as tits and titmice (Paridae). In this way, suspended feeders can provide an added spectacle at the bird table.*

WHAT TO FEED BIRDS

As warm-blooded or endothermic animals, birds have to expend considerable energy maintaining an even body temperature. This process is particularly costly in terms of energy in cold weather, so when temperatures drop toward freezing point, providing food for birds is especially important.

Birds, like many wild creatures, enjoy a range of foods, many of which are easy to obtain. Leftovers are a valuable but variable commodity, so don't rely on them. Seed is useful and can be supplemented with such items as pinhead oatmeal or porridge oats, sultanas, shredded suet and toasted breadcrumbs. Other popular items for the bird table include canned sweetcorn and fresh fruit, broken into pieces.

The more different food types can be left in different positions and types of feeder, the better. Whatever you decide to place out for the birds, make sure that you stick to natural foods, rather than chemically altered or processed items, such as margarine. Keep food fresh – only leave out enough for a day or two – and never allow food or feeding debris to accumulate because it can rapidly spread disease.

FAT PRODUCTS
The best types of base for fat cakes are lamb and beef fats, either in natural form or as processed suet. Because these are

Below: *A live feeder can help a variety of birds, including robins and bluebirds, that rely on prey to feed their young.*

Above: *Half a coconut filled with seeds and melted fat is a good way of providing supplementary food for small, clinging birds.*

hard, they do not melt too readily in warm weather, which can potentially glue birds' beaks together. Specialist manufacturers add enticements to their fat cakes but you can easily make your own at home with a mixture of seeds, fruits and nuts following the recipes on the next pages.

LIVE FOOD
Some birds, robins and bluebirds in particular, can benefit from supplements of live food, such as waxworms and mealworms, particularly during the late winter period when food is scarce and their breeding cycle begins. The worms can easily be purchased from pet shops or by mail order, and can be placed on tables or in specialist feeders.

SEEDS AND GRAINS
Use best-quality seeds from a reliable source, not sweepings or waste seeds as these are neither of interest nor of nutritional value to the birds. Black sunflower seeds rather than the striped

variety are the favoured food of many species. The skins of this type are the thinnest of all sunflower varieties, making them easy for the birds to open. All types of sunflower seeds are safe for young birds to eat, so they may be offered all year round. Canary seeds, melon seeds, hemp seeds, small wheat, kibbled and flaked maize, corn kernels and oatmeal are all good sources of nutrition. The exact mixture of seeds you put out can be fine-tuned to attract particular species of birds to your garden. You could consult a specialist catalogue for more details.

UNSALTED PEANUTS
Buy only high-quality 'safe nuts', marked as such by a reputable ornithological organization or similar body, to ensure that the nuts are free from lethal toxins. Whole peanuts are best avoided during the nesting season because of the danger they pose to nestlings. They should be placed in a mesh peanut feeder from which adult birds can take only small fragments.

Below: *A string of peanuts provides nutrition and can also look attractive if hung in a well-chosen site such as this.*

COMMON BIRD FOODS

The variety of seed and other food supplements that are commonly available in the shops for birds has increased vastly in the last few years. All have their own merits and will be preferred by different types of birds. Trial and error will show what goes down best with the feathered population in your local area, but here are some ideas.

Mixed seed
Consists of various seed types for a wide range of birds, but can be of variable quality.

Black sunflower seed
More commonly known as the 'oil sunflower', this seed – as its name suggests – is rich in oil and ideal for winter-feeding a range of garden birds.

Striped sunflower seed
This type of seed has a lower oil content than the black variety, and is useful in the spring when natural foods become more abundant.

Niger
Sometimes called thistle seed, this tiny black birdseed, cultivated in Asia and Africa, is high in calories and oil content, and is quickly devoured, especially by finches of various types.

Grain
Consists of any commercially grown crops in the grass family, including wheat, millet, maize and oats.

Bread
This is eaten by many species. Brown bread is best, but whatever type you offer, make sure that it has been thoroughly soaked to avoid the danger of it swelling in birds' stomachs.

Dried and fresh fruit
Always popular, dried fruit should be soaked as for bread. Fresh fruits, especially pears and apples, are enjoyed by blackcaps and thrushes. These fruits are particularly useful in winter.

Half-coconut
Hanging on a string, a half-coconut offers good value for money and provides delightful entertainment when acrobatic tits come to feed. Once the flesh has been stripped, the shell can be filled with wholesome bird pudding, a mixture of nuts, seeds and melted fat.

Fat ball
A ball of suet into which other dried foodstuffs have been incorporated. It is usually hung in nets or special feeders.

Suet cake
The block type of suet food contains a mixture of seeds that provides a balanced diet for many species. It is ideal for feeding birds when you are away, although the fat content can sometimes attract scavenging mammals, such as rats, to a table.

Fruit suet treats
Mainly for bird tables or feeders, this suet-based cake is best made with moist, dried fruit and peanut granules, and is popular with larger birds.

Dried mealworms
These freeze-dried grubs are an excellent source of protein for carnivorous birds.

Peanuts
In their shells, peanuts can be strung on thread or wire, but don't use multistranded thread as birds may get their feet caught in this. Do ensure the nuts are fresh – mouldy ones produce a toxin which kills many garden birds.

Hazelnuts
Wedged into tree bark, hazelnuts will appeal to nuthatches, which will enjoy hammering them open.

Cheese
Grated cheese is a popular food with some types of songbirds.

Leftovers
Household foods such as hard-boiled eggs, baked potatoes, uncooked pastry and stale cake and biscuits (cookies) are all widely available choices that birds will enjoy. Feel free to experiment, taking care not to offer dehydrated, spicy or salty foods, as these can be dangerous.

Grit for digestion
Although not actually foodstuffs, grit, sand and gravel aid digestion, particularly for seed-eaters.

Mixed seed

Black sunflower seeds

Niger

Dried fruit

Fresh fruit

Fat ball

Suet cake

Fruit suet treats

Dried mealworms

Peanuts

Cheese

Leftovers

NEST BOXES

In recent years, nest boxes have become a familiar sight in many gardens, chiefly because people like to see birds raising their young. Nest boxes have proved extremely valuable for a variety of birds because they provide alternative, artificial nesting sites for many species.

Before you erect a nest box, decide what type of bird you are trying to help. Different species have different needs. Choosing the wrong type of box or putting it up in an inappropriate place may mean that it is not used. If a box is to be used immediately, it needs to be in place by the start of the breeding season, and that usually means late winter. However, there is never a wrong time of year to put one up, and they often provide winter shelter. A box so used is more likely to be used again next season.

READY-MADE BOXES

There has been a rapid increase in the range of commercially produced bird boxes, and numerous designs are now available to suit a range of garden birds from martins and swifts, owls and woodpeckers, to starlings, sparrows and titmice. Small-scale specialist producers of bird boxes can be found on the Internet.

   The best designs are usually solid and simple. In general, beware fussy, overly ornate boxes, as they can be useless. If you are buying a box, it needs to be waterproof, but it must have a drainage

Below: *Some birds that nest in groups, such as these purple martins* (Progne subis), *will use communal nest boxes.*

Above: *A parent bird, such as this blue tit, feeding a brood of newly hatched chicks is a wonderfully rewarding sight in a garden.*

Above: *Doves roost in dovecotes with ledged entrances. However, in general, an outside ledge can attract predators.*

hole in the bottom to allow any water that blows or seeps in to escape. If there's any standing water, it will make the box cold, might lead to disease, and will increase the chances of rotting the box. For the same reason, make sure that the base of the box is inside the sides and not fixed to the bottom or water will seep straight into the base. The lid must fit tightly,

preferably with a hooked catch to prevent predators, such as squirrels or cats, from getting in and eating the chicks. Boxes with a perch under the entrance hole should be regarded with caution, as they can be used by hungry (predatory) squirrels to stand on. Lastly, avoid using any boxes that have been heavily treated with preservative. The fumes will be off-putting to birds, and what is more, they could prove poisonous to the adults or chicks.

   When you buy bird boxes, make sure that they are accompanied with instructions and other useful information regarding their positioning to maximize the chances of birds taking up residence. The best brands may also offer advice on how you can improve your garden to suit particular species. Buying a bird box from a reputable supplier is probably the simplest (if most expensive) way to achieve success.

FIXING A BIRD BOX

It is not difficult to fix a bird box, but choosing the right position is important. It must be fixed securely so that it doesn't fall when occupied, particularly when well-grown nestlings become more active.

DIFFERENT TYPES OF NEST BOX

There is no standard design for a bird box. What birds really need is a secure and weatherproof home, safe from predators.

Do remember, though, that different bird species have different preferences regarding the type and location of a box.

Enclosed box This style of nest box has a small, usually circular entrance hole. An enclosed box will suit many species, including sparrows, chickadees, titmice, bluebirds, wrens, nuthatches, house finches and woodpeckers. The size of the box and the size and shape of the entrance hole varies with the species you intend to attract. Small birds, such as titmice and chickadees, need relatively small boxes with round holes about 2.8cm/1⅛in wide, while larger birds, such as woodpeckers and owls, need larger boxes with holes that are 6cm/2¼in or more across.

Open-front box Some birds, including European robins, wrens, wagtails and thrushes, will use a nest box with a large, rectangular entrance hole for nesting. The opening width varies accordingly.

Nesting shelf Song sparrows, American robins, and phoebes will use a box with an entirely open front – also called a roosting box – for resting. Barn swallows, blue jays, and cardinals also roost in this style of box.

Duck house Usually large and square, these are attached to poles sunk in water to keep predators away. The rectangular entrance is reached via a ramplike ladder.

Communal box Birds such as purple martins, starlings, and house sparrows form communal nests. In the case of house sparrows, these are commonly sited under the eaves of houses. However, modern energy efficiency means that many former nest sites have been sealed off, and house sparrows often have difficulty in breeding. Communal nest boxes can help to boost numbers of these species.

Swallow nest cup Swallows may have difficulty finding nest sites, and the smooth walls of modern buildings often cause nests to fall, sometimes with the young inside. Near roads, vibration caused by heavy vehicles may also shake nests loose. Artificial nests, made of a wood and cement mix, are sometimes supplied attached to an artificial overhang ready for use.

Owl box These vary considerably in their design and are often more of a tube rather than a box. Smaller owl boxes are used by other large birds because they are often at least three times the size of a standard bird box. There are many designs, but all need a well-drained floor and easy access for cleaning at the end of the season, and are best placed in a large tree in the lower to mid canopy.

Enclosed box | Open-fronted box | Duck house | Communal box | Swallow nest cup | Owl box

Although boxes can be fixed at 1.8m/6ft above ground, they can be placed higher than this, and a height of 3.7m/12ft or more will defeat many predators.

When positioning a bird box, make sure that it is protected from prevailing cold winds and hot sun, preferably giving it a shady aspect or wall that faces away from the strong midday or afternoon sun. Try to ensure that the birds have a fairly clear flight path to and from the nest, and try to angle the box slightly downward to help exclude rain. Remember that birds are often territorial and, in most cases, don't like being crowded together. Leave some space between the boxes unless providing for communal species such as sparrows. There may be natural possibilities already in your garden that, with a little thought, can

be turned into good nest sites. Birds may nest in an old shed that has had the door left purposely ajar, or make their homes in a hole in the eaves of a house or outbuilding.

MAINTENANCE

Inspect the box in late summer or early autumn, and remove any nest material or other debris. This helps reduce parasites. You could add some clean straw if you want small birds to use it over winter. In late winter, clear the box out again ready for the nesting season. Finally, provide nesting materials such as string, cloth, wool, dried grass and excess hair from your cat or dog.

Right: *If you find a nestling on the ground, leave it alone. The parents will not be far away, and may abandon it if you intervene.*

FEEDING TIMES AND BOX LOCATIONS

When providing tables, feeders and nest boxes in your garden, it helps to understand birds' daily rituals and preferred feeding times and food types so that you can get the best results. It is also important to choose appropriate sites for your nest boxes, to maximize their safe use and minimize aggression.

Common feathered visitors in the UK include the blackbird, house sparrow, blue tit, robin, chaffinch, greenfinch, magpie, tree sparrow, collared dove, wren and dunnock, while in North America, cardinals, juncos, titmice, chickadees, finches, mourning doves and American robins will pay regular visits to gardens.

Migration makes for interesting changes. At the end of winter some of your regulars will return to the countryside or migrate to more suitable breeding grounds. You may suddenly notice the odd bird that has never visited your garden before: it may be looking for food to fuel its long journey, or it may have been swept off course. In the winter there will be many visitors looking for food, but during spring the battle for territory will begin, limiting the number of birds in your garden.

DAILY RITUALS

Birds wake up just before dawn, when they sing with great gusto. This dawn chorus involves many different species and lasts about half an hour, heralding the daylight.

Breakfast is the best time to observe birds' behaviour, as they often quarrel over food. You will soon start to notice their

Below: *Many bird species enjoy eating from bird tables, particularly if there are trees nearby, and their playful behaviour is always entertaining to watch.*

pecking order. The first birds to visit the garden may be blackbirds and thrushes, who come to scan the lawn in search of worms and soft grubs. They hunt quietly and carefully, pausing between hops and watching for their prey. Starlings, who arrive later, appear to stab here and there at the ground until they find a tasty morsel.

Birds have two important daily activities. The first is to find and eat food, which is done throughout the day; the second is to take care of their feathers. These must be kept in perfect condition for both flight and insulation. After bathing comes preening. Birds collect fatty oil from

Above: *Though wonderful to watch, fledglings must learn to survive, so any human intervention is not a good idea.*

the preen gland at their rump and smear it over the feathers before stroking them back into place.

WHAT TO FEED WHEN

Birds will quickly come to depend on your support, so once you have enticed them into the garden, you need to make sure that they continue to thrive. It is important to maintain supplies of food and water through the winter. Birds will appreciate fresh food on the table early in the morning, or at least at a regular time. If you go away, fill your feeder and leave fat balls to sustain the birds until your return.

Birds need food with a high fat and carbohydrate content, as they may lose up to 10 per cent of their body weight overnight in bad weather, so suet, cheese, bacon rinds and dripping will help them build up their energy reserves. Crows, starlings, titmice and woodpeckers are particularly attracted to bacon rind, fat and cheese.

The shape of a bird's beak roughly indicates its diet. Finches have hard, thick beaks which are designed to crack and crush. They feed mostly on grain and seed.

Above: *Take care that nest boxes are mounted high enough on trees so that there is no danger of animals, such as cats, reaching the box, especially when there is a ledge attached to the outside.*

Robins and wrens, with their slender, soft beaks, eat caterpillars, grubs and other insects. Gulls, starlings and blackbirds have general-purpose bills, which allow them to eat a bit of everything. Whatever the species, they all enjoy culinary variety, and kitchen scraps are always welcome.

Bread is the food most commonly put out for birds, but it is not particularly good for them. If you do give it, soak it first in water or, even better, fat. In fact any dried foods – especially fruits – should be soaked. Never give birds desiccated coconut or uncooked rice. These swell up in their stomachs and can kill. Kitchen leftovers such as baked potatoes and spaghetti are good: they are soft enough for birds to eat but difficult for them to pick up whole to fly away with. Keep some of your windfall apples and pears in storage until winter, when they will be most welcome on the bird table. Don't worry if birds don't visit your feeder immediately – it may take up to two weeks for a bird table to be accepted by the neighbourhood bird population.

SITING AND MAINTAINING BOXES

When choosing sites for your birdhouse and other accessories, there are several points to bear in mind. Will birds be left in

Above: *Feeders containing either seeds or peanuts can be used to attract small, agile birds to your garden. Food supplies will be especially welcome to these birds during the cold winter months.*

peace there? It's not a good idea to erect a table, nest box or birdbath where children play or where the pet cat tends to prowl. Birds must have shelter nearby to which they can flee if danger threatens.

Place nest boxes so that they are protected from the prevailing wind, rain and strong sunlight. If you put a box on a tree, notice which side of the trunk has more algae growing. This will be the wet side, so place the box on the opposite side. If you angle the box slightly forward it will give more shelter to the occupants.

Be careful not to damage the tree by banging nails into it; special securing devices are available for this purpose. Boxes don't have to be rigidly mounted, as long as they are secure. Boxes that hang from a wire or string work well and may offer better protection from predators such as cats and squirrels.

The best time of year to put up nest boxes is in the autumn. They can then act as roosts during the winter and be ready for early spring when the birds start choosing their breeding sites. During the winter you can insulate them with cotton, straw or wood shavings for roosting birds, but remember to remove this padding before nesting begins in the spring. Cleaning out birdhouses and nest boxes after the

breeding season is very important. Wash the boxes out with mild disinfectant diluted with plenty of water. Always wear rubber gloves to protect yourself from any parasites that may be lurking inside.

If birds do nest in your boxes, don't be tempted to sneak a look – the shock may cause the mother to abandon her brood or the young chicks to leave their nest prematurely. The best help you can give nesting birds is to leave them undisturbed.

AVOIDING AGGRESSION

To discourage fighting, don't overdo the number of boxes you set up in your garden. Robins and titmice can be very territorial and aggressive with other members of their own species. A bird's territory is a fixed area that it will defend for either feeding or breeding or both. If a bird does not manage to establish its territory it will be unable to nest or breed, and may even die of hunger. The gestures birds make to communicate with each other are known as displays.

To show aggression, a bird will puff up its feathers, raise its wings and point its beak at its rival to look menacing. To show submission, a bird will crouch down and sleek its feathers in. Fights most commonly occur when a newcomer arrives in the territory of an established group, and the stranger's status needs to be evaluated. Occasionally, birds will fight to the death.

Below: *Water can be provided for birds in small gardens by hanging up bowls or attaching containers or troughs to a wall.*

BUILDING MATERIALS

Bird boxes, feeders and baths for garden species can be constructed using a wide variety of materials. The garden shed will probably provide many suitable items, such as sticks, string, garden wire, paint, varnish and offcuts of wood. You may be able to improvise using materials not listed here.

ALUMINIUM MESH
Useful for making bird feeders, this is available from hardware shops and some hobby suppliers. Birds can peck food through a coarse mesh, while a fine gauze can be used to line the base of a feeder to enable rain to drain away.

CLAY
A birdhouse moulded from potter's clay will need to be fired in a kiln. Self-hardening clay does not need firing, and is available in various colours, including stone and terracotta. You will need to varnish the clay to make it water-resistant.

COCONUT
Birds love fresh coconut, and when they have eaten the contents you can use the half shells as parts of a birdhouse or fill them with bird pudding. Never put out dry, shredded coconut.

CORRUGATED ROOFING MATERIAL
Any offcut that you are able to purchase from a DIY shop would be enough to cover a large birdhouse. You will need to buy special screws to attach it.

Below: Paintbrushes will be useful for decorating projects. You will need medium-sized brushes as well as very fine ones.

Above: *Hanging basket liners can be purchased in various colours, including green, which blends with garden settings.*

HANGING BASKET LINERS
Basket liners are available in a soft green with a texture that resembles moss. They can be cut to size and moulded over chicken wire.

PAINT AND VARNISH
Use exterior quality paint with a satin or matt finish. If you use emulsion paint, it will need to be protected with a varnish designed for exterior use, such as yacht varnish. For fine work, use craft enamels or artist's acrylics.

PAINTBRUSHES
You will need a range of small household paintbrushes, together with medium and fine artist's brushes for detailed decoration. Clean brushes in white spirit if you are using oil-based paints.

PALETTE
A white ceramic tile, or an old plate, is useful for mixing paint colours.

READY-MADE BIRDHOUSES
As an alternative to making your own birdhouse, you can buy ready-made houses inexpensively and customize them to suit the style of your garden.

Above: *Shells provide a decorative finish to projects. Collect them responsibly – by recycling old necklaces, for example.*

ROOFING SLATES AND TILES
Beautiful old roofing slates and tiles can often be purchased from architectural salvage yards and make excellent weatherproof roofs for birdhouses.

SELF-ADHESIVE ROOF FLASHING
This material is tough and waterproof. It looks like lead and makes an invaluable covering for birdhouse roofs.

SHELLS
These make pretty decorations. You can buy them from craft shops or, better still, use an old shell necklace.

STICKS
Garden canes are available in a range of colours. Thick stakes can be used to support some houses. Withes are willow stems used for weaving. They are available stripped or unstripped, and become very pliable once soaked. Straight hazel twigs can be gathered in the garden or hedge.

STRING
Ordinary household string is useful for many projects, as well as for hanging up feeders. Green garden string and natural raffia make good binding materials and

garden string has also usually been treated for outdoor use to help it last longer. Sea grass string is both strong and decorative.

WIRE

Plastic-coated chicken wire is attractive and easy to work with, as it will not scratch your hands. Garden wire is also plastic-coated and comes in various gauges. Galvanized wire is useful for constructing and suspending birdhouses. Florist's wire is much thinner and is useful for binding.

WOOD

For long-lasting, weatherproof houses, use timber that is at least 15mm/⅝in thick. Planed pine is easily available in a wide range of widths. For outdoor use, treat it with preservative, or paint or varnish it. Tongue and groove or ship-lap boards make attractive walls for larger birdhouses. Marine or exterior quality plywood is easy to cut with a fretsaw for decorative panels. A birdhouse made from a hollowed-out log looks good in natural surroundings.

Clockwise from top left: *Natural and planed wood, a ready-made birdhouse, natural and treated willow, aluminium mesh and wire sheets, galvanized and plastic-coated wire, a range of paints, paintbrushes, string, liner, roof slate, coconut, self-adhesive flashing, clay, sticks and shells.*

BUILDING EQUIPMENT

No special equipment is needed for building bird boxes and feeders, and only basic carpentry skills will be required. Take care when using new equipment; you might like to practise on a scrap first. Before cutting, always recheck against the template, or double-check your measurements.

ADHESIVES
Glue all joints in wooden birdhouses, using wood glue, before nailing or screwing them together. Masking tape can be useful for holding wood together while glue is drying. Two-part epoxy resin glue makes a strong bond when you are joining disparate materials. Small stones or shells can be embedded in ready-mixed tile cement for a decorative finish. Always use exterior grade glue, especially when you are working with PVA (white) glue.

BROWN PAPER
Heavy craft paper makes a good protective covering for your work surface when painting or gluing. Old newspaper is also ideal as protective covering.

CRAFT KNIFE AND SCISSORS
Always use a sharp blade in a craft knife and protect the work surface with a cutting mat. When using self-adhesive flashing, cut with a sharp knife, rather than scissors.

DRILL AND BITS
A drill will be needed to make holes for screws and other fixings. Spade bits can be used to make entry holes up

Below: Drill holes using a clamp to keep your work steady. If you use countersink screws, you will need a countersink bit.

Above: *Glue can be spread using a gun, simple spatula or even a matchstick. Wipe off any excess glue before it dries.*

to 2.5cm/1in. Hole saws, which fit on to a drill, are available in a range of sizes to cut larger entry holes for birdhouses. You can also cut an entry hole using a fretsaw and jigsaw, if a hole saw is not available.

GLOVES
Wear gardening gloves to protect yourself from scratches when you are handling, bending or cutting wire. You could wear

Below: Pliers will be useful to bend and mould wire, and also to cut it. Protect your hands by wearing thick gloves.

Above: *Hammer steadily and gently, taking care to keep your free hand well away from the hammer head.*

a pair of rubber gloves to keep your hands clean whenever you are painting or varnishing, or using modelling clay.

HAMMER AND NAILS
Use galvanized nails or plated moulding pins, which will not rust.

PENCIL AND RULERS
Use a sharp pencil and ruler for accurate marking out of wood. Use a metal ruler when cutting with a craft knife.

PLIERS AND CUTTERS
General-purpose pliers and small, round-nosed ones will be useful for working with wire. You will also need wire cutters. Lead flashing, for roofs, can be cut using tin snips.

SANDPAPER
Smooth the edges of the wood after cutting using medium-grade sandpaper wrapped around a wooden block. Roll a piece of sandpaper around your finger to smooth the edges of entry holes.

SAWS
Use a tenon saw for square cutting, unless you are making large cuts, in which case you will need a panel saw. Curved shapes can

be cut using a jigsaw. Use a fretsaw to cut small, intricate shapes. When cutting, you should always support the wood on a V-board screwed to the workbench. Use a hacksaw to cut metal.

SCREWS AND SCREWDRIVER

Screws rather than nails should be used to make secure fixings in large, heavy structures. Buy Pozidriv screws for outdoor use, as these tend to be plated and therefore will be less inclined to rust.

VICE AND CLAMPS

A vice or adjustable workbench will be essential for holding wood steady when you are sawing it, and can also help when you are gluing. A bench hook will be helpful when you are cutting timber with a tenon saw, because it is useful for cutting strips to length. You will need to clamp a coconut in a vice to saw it in half. Clamps of various sizes, and even clothes pegs can be useful for holding your work together while you are assembling it.

Clockwise from top left: *Sandpaper and wooden blocks, panel and tenon saw, drill kit and bits, brown paper, hacksaw, paintbrushes, pencil and ruler, craft knife and masking tape, scissors, pliers and cutters, screwdriver and screws, hammers and nails, epoxy resin glue, wood glue and spatula, rubber and fabric gloves and vice.*

FEEDERS AND BIRDBATHS

Many species of garden birds have suffered quite serious declines in recent years. By providing food and water you will help your local bird population to remain fit and healthy, so that the birds are more likely to breed successfully. As well as seeds, nuts and fruit, birds need a constant supply of water, for both bathing and drinking. The projects on the following pages include wire hanging feeders, coconut feeders, bottle feeders, bird tables and willow feeders, as well as copper and chrome birdbaths.

Left: *Small perching birds, such as this juvenile great tit, are able to take advantage of hanging feeders, safe from competition.*

Above: *From rudimentary woodwork to more complex projects, bird-feeder construction can suit every skill level.*

Above: *Simple feeders such as this one look very attractive when filled with foods with different colours and textures.*

Above: *Pieces of broken crockery make a wonderful mosaic pattern. The sloping sides provide easy access to the water.*

WIRE BIRD FEEDER

Small aluminium drinks cans and aluminium mesh form the basis for these simple feeders which, when filled with seeds or peanuts, will attract a range of species, including tits.

1 Cut a small aluminium drink can in half, then draw a decorative scalloped border around each half and cut out using scissors. Trim off any jagged edges.

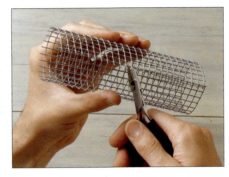

2 Cut a rectangle of mesh to fit, rolled up, inside the can. Roll the mesh around a bottle. Join the edges by hooking the cut ends through and bending them with pliers.

3 Pierce a hole in the bottom of the can. Fit the mesh cylinder into the two halves of the can, then thread them on to galvanized wire. Twist the lower end of the wire into a flat coil so that the feeder cannot slide off.

4 Leave enough wire above the top so you can slide the top off for refilling, then allow an extra 7.5cm/3in. Cut the wire. Twist the end into a flat coil, then make a hook by bending the wire over a marker pen.

YOU WILL NEED
small aluminium drink cans
old scissors, wire cutters
aluminium mesh
straight-sided bottle
small pliers and bradawl or awl
galvanized wire
permanent marker pen

TYPICAL FOOD
peanuts, sunflower seeds

TYPICAL VISITORS
tits, titmice and chickadees
woodpeckers and finches

Above: *Woodpeckers are well-suited to taking nuts from wire feeders, with their long, straight bills and powerful claws.*

BOUNTY BOWER

In winter, the food you provide can make the difference between life and death for birds. Once you have started, continue to put food out each day, but for a real treat offer this gourmet selection.

1 Skewer an apple and thread it on to a long piece of garden wire. Wind the end around the base of the apple to prevent it slipping off. Embed sunflower seeds into the flesh of the apple. You can adjust the quantities to suit the number of birds that call at your bower.

2 Screw metal eyelets into the base of a selection of pine cones. Thread them with string and tie the cones together in size order. Hang the string on an existing bower.

3 Tie a selection of millet bunches with raffia. Using a darning needle and strong thread, thread unshelled peanuts to make long strings. Saw a coconut in half. Drill two holes near the edge of one half and thread a piece of wire through them. Twist the ends of the wire together.

4 When the seeds have been pecked out of the cones, you can revamp them by filling with unsalted, unroasted smooth peanut butter and dipping in small mixed seeds.

YOU WILL NEED
skewer
garden wire
wire cutters
metal eyelets
string
scissors
raffia
darning needle
strong thread
hacksaw
drill
unsalted, unroasted smooth peanut
    butter (from health food shops)

TYPICAL FOOD
apple
millet bunches
whole coconut
peanuts in their shells
sunflower seeds
mixed birdseed
niger (thistle)
pine cones

TYPICAL VISITORS
finches and grosbeaks
titmice and chickadees
blue jays

COCONUT FEEDER

A plastic tube, made from a recycled cosmetic bottle, makes a practical seed-dispenser. The half-coconut roof lifts off to the side, allowing you to refill the plastic tube. Tits are particularly adept at using this kind of feeder and their acrobatics can be entertaining.

Above: *Finches, such as goldfinches, grosbeaks, siskins, and this house finch (Carpodacus mexicanus), often visit feeders. Separate populations of house finches exist in different parts of the United States. Redpolls will also use feeders such as this.*

YOU WILL NEED
2 coconuts
drill
hole saw
knife
hacksaw
4cm/1½in diameter straight-sided
    plastic bottle
scissors
florist's wire
twigs
small pliers
string
bead

TYPICAL FOOD
sunflower seeds
mixed seed

TYPICAL VISITORS
finches
redpolls
robins and sparrows
tits and titmice

1 Drill two holes in the top of each coconut and drain the milk. Cut two 5cm/2in holes from one on opposite sides and a third at the top. Remove the flesh with a knife.

3 Beneath each large side hole in the first coconut, drill two tiny holes on either side. These will be used for holding the perches. Drill two further holes on each side for attaching the roof.

5 Attach a perch beneath each side hole by threading florist's wire through the small drilled holes and around a twig, twisting it to form a cross over the centre. Using small pliers, twist the ends of the wire together inside the coconut to secure it.

2 Saw the second coconut in half. Remove the flesh from one half to form the roof of the feeder. Make a small hole in the top and two holes on each side near the rim.

4 Remove the top and bottom of a plastic bottle to make a tube. Cut two semicircles at the bottom on opposite sides to allow seeds to spill out. Place the tube in the first coconut through the large hole at the top.

6 Attach the roof to the base by threading string through the side holes in the coconuts. Tie a bead to a doubled piece of string, to act as an anchor, and thread the string through the central hole of the roof for hanging the feeder.

BOTTLE FEEDER

This elegant and practical seed feeder keeps the contents dry. You will be able to regulate the flow of seed by adjusting the height of the bottle, but don't forget to cover the opening while you insert the filled bottle into the frame, to avoid spilling any seed.

Above: *Sparrows, such as song sparrows, are among the most common visitors to seed feeders. In recent years, some types of sparrows have declined, but putting out seeds for them can help reverse the trend.*

YOU WILL NEED
bottle
pierced galvanized metal L-shaped
    bracket
hacksaw (if needed)
galvanized wire
pliers
13cm/5in tart tin with
    removable base
aluminium gauze
old scissors
epoxy resin glue
florist's wire

TYPICAL FOOD
black sunflower seeds
striped sunflower seeds
mixed seed

TYPICAL VISITORS
blue tits, great tits and titmice
sparrows
finches
dunnocks and siskins
juncos

1 Measure your chosen bottle against the metal bracket and, if the bracket is too long, cut off the excess metal using a hacksaw. However, it does not matter if a little of the bracket shows above the top.

2 Cut a piece of wire long enough to wrap around the bottle in a criss-cross fashion. Thread both ends of the wire through an appropriate hole positioned near the top of the bracket.

3 Place the bottle in position on the bracket and wrap the wire around it, forming a criss-cross shape. Secure the wire by threading it through a hole on the bracket at the back.

4 Repeat the process at the neck of the bottle, so that the bottle is held in place by two lots of crossed wire. Twist the ends of the wire together at the back of the bracket using a pair of pliers.

5 Remove the bottle from the frame, fill with seeds and set aside. Remove the bottom of the tart tin and use it as a template to cut out a circular piece of aluminium gauze. Glue the gauze into the bottom of the tin.

6 Using florist's wire, attach the tin to the bracket by wiring through the gauze. Add the filled bottle. The gap between the bottle neck and the pan should be wide enough to let seeds trickle through.

RUSTIC BIRD TABLE

A basic table is one of the simplest ways of dispensing food to birds. One of the advantages is that it can take many different kinds of food. You can make this attractive rustic table quite simply from two pieces of rough wood, nailed together with battens to strengthen the structure. The lip around the edge is designed to stop nuts and seeds rolling off. String is tied to a hook in each corner so that the table can be hung in a tree, out of reach of predators.

Above: *Finches, such as the chaffinch (*Fringilla coelebs*), shown here, and* purple finch *(Carpodacus purpureus) are among the species that benefit from bird tables.*

YOU WILL NEED
rough wood, 25 x 13 x 1cm/
    10 x 5 x ½in (x 2)
battens, 25 x 2.5 x 2.5cm/
    10 x 1 x 1in (x 2) and
    28 x 5 x 1cm/11 x 2 x ½in
    (x 4)
nails
hammer
wood preservative
paintbrush
4 brass hooks
2m/2yd sisal string
scissors

TYPICAL FOOD
varied, including seeds, bread

TYPICAL VISITORS
finches and cardinals
sparrows and juncos
tits and titmice

1 Join together the two pieces of rough wood by positioning them side by side and placing the two 25cm/10in battens across the wood, one at each end. Nail the battens securely in place to make the base.

2 Nail the four 28cm/11in lengths of batten around the edges of the flat side of the table, creating a lip of at least 2.5cm/1in. This will ensure the food is not spilled.

3 Lightly paint all the surfaces of the table with wood preservative and leave to dry.

4 Screw a brass hook into each corner of the table to attach the string.

5 Cut the sisal string into four equal lengths and tie a small loop in one end of each piece. Attach each loop to a hook, then gather up the strings above the table and tie in a loop for hanging.

KITCHEN BIRD TABLE

This original bird table uses cooking and cleaning equipment in ingenious ways, and makes an offbeat sculpture at the same time. The sieves allow rain to drain away, and the finial is the head of a balloon whisk, into which a fat ball can be inserted.

1 Clamp the sieve handle under a wooden block and bend it through 90 degrees. Then bend it further by hand to fit around the broom handle. Repeat the same process with the other sieves.

2 Nail a piece of scrap wood to the bottom of the broom handle and firmly anchor this in the bucket using large beach pebbles.

3 Position the sieves along the length of the broom handle and hold each one in place by threading a wooden spoon into the bent handle. Once you are happy with the arrangement, sand grooves into the broom for the spoons to fit into.

4 Using either a hacksaw or wire cutters, remove the handle of a balloon whisk and attach it to the top of the broom handle using a length of galvanized wire. This provides a holder for a fat ball.

YOU WILL NEED
clamps
metal sieves (strainers)
wooden block
scrap wood
protective gloves
broom handle
nails
hammer
galvanized bucket
beach pebbles
wooden spoons
sandpaper
balloon whisk
hacksaw or wire cutters
galvanized wire

TYPICAL FOOD
fat ball
sunflower seeds
mixed seed
shelled peanuts
leftovers and kitchen scraps

TYPICAL VISITORS
doves and starlings
thrushes and bluebirds
jays
sparrows
cardinals and chickadees

PALLADIAN BIRD TABLE

This classical-style feeding table looks elegant and impressive but is actually relatively simple to make. It will not only attract birds that enjoy eating seeds, fat and scraps, but will also beautify any garden setting. It can be mounted on a pole, hung from a branch or fixed to a wall using a large bracket.

Above: *The siskin (*Carduelis spinus*), a member of the finch family, can be drawn to bird tables holding seeds and scraps.*

YOU WILL NEED

12mm/½in medium-density fibreboard (MDF) or exterior-grade plywood (for the base)
6mm/¼in medium-density fibreboard (MDF) or exterior-grade plywood
ruler, pencil
saw
glue gun and glue sticks
8 threaded knobs, 30mm/1¼in diameter x 20mm/¾in deep
4 dowels, 120 x 16mm/4¾ x ⅝in
drill and 3mm/⅛in bit
exterior-grade filler
fine-grade sandpaper
medium paintbrush
off-white emulsion (latex) paint
exterior-grade varnish

TYPICAL FOOD
varied, including seeds, fat, scraps

TYPICAL VISITORS
tits and titmice
chickadees, finches and cardinals

1 Mark and cut out all the pieces, following the template given at the back of the book. Assemble the base and steps with wood glue. You could apply hot glue using a glue gun if you possess one.

3 Glue each half of the roof on to the top of the gable triangles. Make sure each roof half overlaps the ceiling by the same amount at the sides and each end.

5 Glue the threaded cupboard knobs in position at each corner mark on the base and the ceiling. Allow to dry thoroughly. Meanwhile drill each end of the dowel columns to accommodate the protruding thread of the knobs.

2 Mark the positions of the columns at each corner of the top step and on the underside of the ceiling. Glue the main gable triangles in place on each end of the ceiling piece.

4 Allow enough time for the roof glue to dry thoroughly. Next, glue the decorative gable triangle in place centrally on the face of the front gable.

6 Apply glue to each thread and assemble the dowels between the base and the roof. Fill any gaps with exterior-grade filler. Rub down with fine-grade sandpaper and paint with off-white emulsion (latex) followed by several coats of exterior-grade varnish.

SEASIDE BIRD TABLE

The pretty decorative details and distressed paintwork of this bird table are reminiscent of seaside architecture. You can use plain dowelling – or a broom handle – to make the supports for the roof, or recycle the turned legs from an old piece of furniture.

Above: *European starlings* (Sturnus vulgaris) *have spread across North America since being introduced from the Old World.*

1 Using the templates, mark out the base, roof base and roof ends on pine board. Cut out using a jigsaw. Drill a 2cm/¾in hole in each corner of the two bases. Glue and screw the roof ends to the roof base.

2 In the base, drill a starter hole for the fretsaw. Cut out a 7.5cm/3in diameter hole, 5cm/2in in from one short side. Glue the four dowelling supports in place on the frame and base. Leave to dry overnight.

YOU WILL NEED
2cm/¾in pine board
pencil, ruler
jigsaw or scroll saw
drill
wood glue
4 screws
screwdriver
fretsaw
4 x 20cm/8in lengths of 2cm/¾in dowelling
4mm/⅙in plywood
sandpaper
plated moulding pins
hammer
watercolour paints
paintbrushes
petroleum jelly
white emulsion (latex) paint
blowtorch
satin yacht varnish
water bowl

TYPICAL FOOD
varied, including kitchen scraps

TYPICAL VISITORS
starlings and robins
sparrows, mockingbirds and juncos
finches and thrushes

3 From the 4mm/⅙in plywood, cut five strips 2.5cm/1in wide for each roof end panel. Cut seven 2.5cm/1in strips for each side of the roof. Cut out the scalloped edging pieces, four strips for the eaves and two lozenges for the finials. Sand surfaces.

4 Glue the plywood strips across the roof ends and nail in place with the pins. Attach the roof slats along the sides of the roof, and the scalloped frills all around the roof edge and the base. A piece of cardboard can hold the pins steady while hammering.

5 Paint the bird table with a dilute mixture of cobalt blue and burnt umber watercolour paint. Leave to dry, then smear on a thin layer of petroleum jelly with your fingers. Apply white emulsion (latex) paint and dry it with a blowtorch to make the paint crack.

6 To age the paintwork, apply a dilute, equal mixture of yellow ochre and burnt sienna watercolours. Leave to dry, then finish with a coat of satin yacht varnish. Attach to a ready-made stand and place a water bowl on the table.

BAMBOO BIRD TABLE

It is a real treat to watch birds feeding, and seeing them at close range from the comfort of your armchair is even better. This bamboo structure is designed to hang on a wall from two cup hooks. Position it near a window so that you can see the birds easily.

Above: *With his bright pink chest, the male bullfinch (*Pyrrhula pyrrhula*) is one of the most attractive members of the finch family. The female has duller plumage.*

YOU WILL NEED
tenon saw
wood offcut
pencil
ruler
drill
bamboo canes
clips
garden string
scissors
scrap roofing material
baking tin
2 clothes pegs
wire whisk

TYPICAL FOOD
fat ball
peanuts in their shells
sunflower seeds
breadcrumbs
kitchen scraps

TYPICAL VISITORS
tits and titmice
finches and juncos
jays and mockingbirds

1 Mark and cut out a rectangle 12 x 16cm/ 4½ x 6¼in on the wood offcut. Drill a hole in each corner and push in four 90cm/36in canes. Cut two short lengths of cane and clip them diagonally at the top to hold the uprights in place.

2 Using the templates at the back of the book as a guide, tie on the horizontal canes, using garden string. These will hold the baking tin firmly on each side. Add two diagonal canes on each side as shown, to reinforce the structure.

3 Tie on the roof supports on each side, again using the templates given at the back of the book as a guide. Use garden string or twine to tie the supports.

4 Join the two sides of the structure, first attaching the bottom diagonal canes, then with two pieces running straight across at the level of the feeding tray.

5 To attach the roof, drill four holes in the roofing sheet. Unclip the top diagonals and push the roof down over the uprights until it is resting on the roof supports. Tie on the long top diagonals.

6 Snip off the long ends of the string and attach the feeding tray with two clothes pegs. Use the top long diagonals to hang food from, such as a whisk as a fat ball holder, or nuts.

RUSTIC FEEDERS

These two feeders in different styles originate from the same basic ready-made model. One has been sanded and given a driftwood-style paint effect, while the other has been camouflaged beneath found objects, including a rusty tin sheet and a short length of plasterer's angle bead.

Above: *With their long, sharp bills, woodpeckers are well equipped to harvest nuts from feeders such as these.*

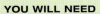

YOU WILL NEED
2 wooden bird feeders
light grey emulsion (latex) paint
medium paintbrushes
sandpaper
clear glue
sand
stub wire
pencil, corks
natural twine
shells, twigs or moss
craft knife or scalpel
thick florist's wire
protective gloves
sheet of old tin
tin snips or saw
glue gun and glue sticks
plasterer's angle bead
black spray paint

TYPICAL FOOD
shelled peanuts

TYPICAL VISITORS
woodpeckers
tits, titmice and finches

1 Paint the first feeder and allow to dry. Rub down with sandpaper to give the surface a weathered, driftwood effect. Apply clear glue to the roof and sprinkle sand over it. Twist lengths of stub wire around a pencil and weave natural twine through them to imitate coils of rope.

3 For the second feeder, wearing protective gloves, snip pieces of old tin to make a roof. Remove all sharp edges and glue in place. Glue moss around the base.

2 Add natural objects found either in the countryside or on the seashore, such as shells, twigs and moss, to decorate and personalize the feeder. Shells can be attached with glue. Use cut-off corks to seal the feed chambers, and tie a loop of florist's wire to suspend the house.

4 Make the roof ridge from plasterer's angle bead sprayed with black paint. Glue it firmly to the house. Plug the feed holes with corks and suspend with wire as before.

Left and right: *Two very different results can be achieved using the same basic ready-made feeder. You can experiment with different materials and applications to create your own designs. You could be very creative with the choice of found objects you use, to give your personalized feeder a flavour of whatever is in its immediate environment. This will help it to harmonize with the garden setting. Or you could use materials such as shells, collected at the seaside, to produce a delightful memento.*

GLASS GAZEBO FEEDER

Constructed from recycled cans and small pieces of glass,
this converted lantern makes a highly attractive feeder, which
will shine, jewel-like, from among the surrounding dark foliage.

1 This lantern required extra glass to be installed. If this is the case, measure the areas required and reduce all measurements by 6mm/¼in to allow for the metal border around each panel. Using a chinagraph pencil, mark the reduced measurements on the glass, then cut out by running a glass cutter in a single pass along a ruler, while pressing firmly. Tap along the score line to break the glass. It is always advisable to wear protective gloves when handling glass.

2 Still wearing gloves, cut 9mm/⅜in strips of metal from a used can using tin snips. Wrap a strip of metal around each edge of each glass panel. Trim, then smear a small amount of soldering flux on to the adjoining surfaces of each corner joint.

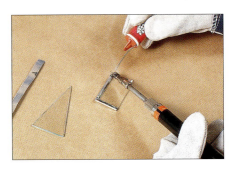

3 Solder the corner joints of each panel. Heat up a joint using a soldering iron and apply solder until it flows between the surfaces to be joined. Remove the heat source. The solder will set in seconds, but the metal will remain hot for some time.

4 Measure openings for the hoppers and fold sections of metal, using a try-square or ruler to keep the folds straight. Solder the meeting points of each hopper. Cut a base from fine wire mesh, then solder the base, panels and hoppers in place.

YOU WILL NEED
glass lantern
tape measure (optional)
thin glass (optional)
chinagraph pencil (optional)
try-square (optional)
glass cutter (optional)
ruler
protective gloves
shiny can (not aluminium),
    washed and dried
tin snips
flux and soldering iron
solder
fine wire mesh

TYPICAL FOOD
shelled peanuts
black sunflower seeds
striped sunflower seeds

TYPICAL VISITORS
tits and titmice
sparrows and juncos
finches, siskins and redpolls
starlings and blue jays

WOVEN WILLOW FEEDER

Made from the supple branches of unstripped willow, this woven basket feeder will look very picturesque placed in the garden. It could be used to dispense foods such as peanuts. The conical roof is packed with moss: as well as adding weight, this will provide valuable nesting material for breeding birds.

Left: *Birds such as jays, finches and this willow warbler (*Phylloscopos trochilus*) will enjoy foraging in this woven willow feeder.*

YOU WILL NEED
about 150 withes
knife or bodkin
clothes peg (pin)
secateurs
bradawl or awl (optional)
pencil or pen, string
6 long strands ivy, moss
glycerine (optional)
garden twine

TYPICAL FOOD
shelled peanuts or seeds

TYPICAL VISITORS
warblers and buntings
jays and finches

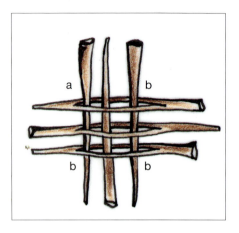

1 Trim six withes to a length of 23cm/9in from the butt (thick) end. Pierce the centre of three of these rods using a knife or bodkin and push the other three withes through them to form a cross. The rods should be arranged with the butt ends pointing in alternate directions. Push the rods together.

2 The cross you have made will form the centre of the base of the feeder. Insert the tips of two long withes into the slits to the left of the short rods and hold them in place by gripping the slit rods. Take one long withe in front of the three uprights, and behind the next three rods. Take the second withe behind the first three rods and in front of the next three, crossing its partner at b. Continue this weave for two complete rounds. Prise the rods apart to form the spokes of a wheel and continue weaving. Try to keep the weaving as tight as possible.

3 Continue to weave the base of the feeder basket, adding new weavers either butt to butt or alternatively tip to tip. The new one is placed to the left of, and under, the old end, which should finish resting on a bottom rod, while the new weaver carries on over it. Join both new weavers at the same time, on neighbouring bottom rods. Continue with your weaving until the base of the basket measures about 18cm/7in, finishing with tips. Temporarily secure the ends with a clothes peg and then trim the bottom rods flush with the weaving.

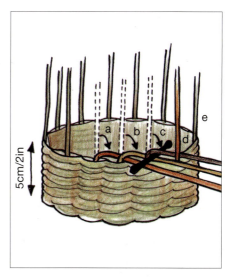

4 Having finished the base, you can now start to fashion the uprights which will support the cone-shaped roof of the bird feeder. Start by selecting 12 new withes. Trim the butt ends of the rods by slicing down the back of each one with a sharp knife, to make a thin wedge-shape. Insert each new willow stick to the left of a bottom rod. You may need to loosen the weave first, using a bodkin or bradawl, before you can fit in the new rod if you have woven the base very tightly.

5 Using your thumb nail or the blade of a knife, make an indentation in each of the new willow sticks where they join the base, then gently bend each one up to form the uprights and temporarily tie them all together at the top with string. You can now start to make the sides of the basket. Begin by inserting three new willow sticks, tip end first, to lie to the right of three consecutive uprights. Take the left-hand weaver in front of two uprights, behind the third and out to the front again.

6 Repeat with the second and third. Continue this pattern, pushing the weavers down, until the side of the basket measures 5cm/2in. Join in new weavers butt to butt or tip to tip, laying the three new rods to the right of the three old rods. To finish the basket, make a kink in each upright over a pencil or pen about twice the diameter of the rod. Bend the first rod (a) behind the second (b) and round to the front. Bend (b) over and behind (c), then bend (c) over and behind (d) and round to the front.

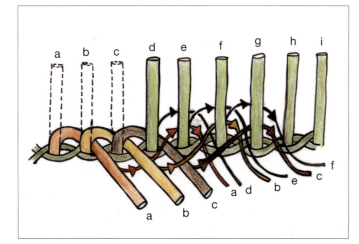

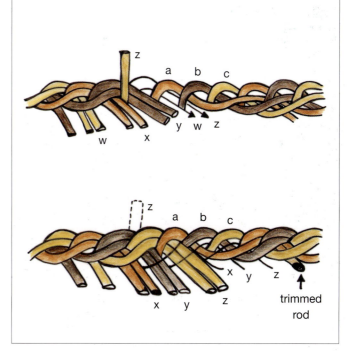

7 To finish off the border: rod (a) travels in front of (c) and (d) and behind (e) and lies in front. (d) bends down and lies beside and to the right of (a). Rod (b) travels in front of (d) and (e) and behind (f) and lies in front. (e) bends over and lies beside and to the right of (b). Rod (c) travels in front of (e) and (f) and behind (g) and lies to the front. Rod (f) lies down beside and to the right of (c). There are now 3 pairs of rods (ad), (be) and (cf). Continue the work always weaving with three pairs of rods until the end of the border. Always start with the far left pair of rods (ad) but use the right-hand rod (d), (e) and (f) and make each rod do the same journey (in front of two uprights, behind one) and pull down the next upright (g), (h) and (i), until there is only one upright left.

8 To finish the border, starting with the far left pair as before, each right-hand rod goes in front of two rods (which are not now upright) and behind the third, coming out through the original 'arches' made with a, b and c. Pull all the rods well down into place, lying tightly together. Trim the ends neatly all round the basket.

9 To make the frame for the roof, select 12 rods and trim them to 30cm/12in. Tie them securely together, 5cm/2in from the tips, using ivy. The ivy can be stripped of its leaves, or you can preserve the leaves by soaking them in glycerine, diluted half and half with water, for several days. Bend a withe into a circle a little larger than the basket. To secure the rods for the roof to the circular frame, take two long ivy stems, stripped of leaves, and tie them to the left of an upright. Wind one length around the upright above the frame and the other around the upright below the frame. Take both pieces around the frame to cross between the first and second uprights, then around the frame to the second upright. Repeat the pattern.

10 Weave the roof using the same pattern as for the sides of the basket using two sets of three rods, then change to a pairing weave, going in front of one upright and behind the next. Near the top, use a single rod weaving in and out and go as high as you can. Stuff the roof with moss.

11 To hold the moss in place, tie garden twine across the base of the roof, connecting each upright with the ones on the opposite side to make a star pattern. Cut four rods 20cm/8in long and trim both ends of each into flat wedges. Push them, equally spaced, into the weave of the roof and into corresponding positions in the basket, using a bodkin to open the weave if necessary.

COPPER BIRDBATH

You will have endless pleasure watching many different species of birds drinking from or preening and cleaning in this beautiful yet eminently practical beaten copper birdbath.

1 Using a chinagraph pencil and a piece of looped string, mark a 45cm/17¾in circle on the 0.9mm/20 SWG copper sheet.

2 Wearing protective gloves, cut out the circle with a pair of tin snips. Carefully smooth any sharp edges using a file.

3 Put the copper on a blanket and hammer it lightly from the centre. Spread the dips out to the rim. Repeat, starting from the centre each time, to get the required shape.

4 Continue hammering until you have achieved a shallow dish shape that will allow birds to enter and leave the water without difficulty. To make the perch, cut 1m/1yd copper wire, loop and hold the ends in a vice. Insert a cup hook into the chuck of a hand drill or slow-speed power drill. Put the cup hook through the loop. Run the drill to twist the wire. Drill three 3mm/⅛in holes around the rim of the bath.

5 Bend a knot into one end of each of three 1m/1yd lengths of wire. Thread the wires through the holes from beneath the bath. Slip the twisted wire over two of the straight wires to form a perch, and hang in a suitable position.

6 Maintain a constant supply of fresh drinking water all year round to help ensure the health of your local bird population. Once the birds have got used to this new feature, many different varieties will visit to bathe and drink.

YOU WILL NEED
chinagraph pencil (china marker)
string
0.9mm/20 SWG copper sheet
protective gloves
tin snips
file
blanket or carpet square
hammer
medium copper wire, 4m/13ft
cup hook
drill and 3mm/⅛in bit

TYPICAL VISITORS
blackbirds
tits and titmice
finches and sparrows

CHROME BIRDBATH

The gently sloping sides of a dustbin lid allow smaller birds to paddle, while larger birds can have a good splash in the middle without emptying the water. A night light fitted under the bath will prevent the water freezing over on winter days.

1 Using a hacksaw, saw across the middle of the dustbin lid handle. Bend back both sides of the severed handle using pliers.

2 Wearing protective gloves, remove the handle from the cheese grater using pliers. Once you have managed to detach one side of the handle from the securing rivet, the other will work free more easily.

YOU WILL NEED
hacksaw
galvanized dustbin (trashcan) lid
pliers
protective gloves
cylindrical metal cheese grater
round fence post to suit size of grater
galvanized nails, hammer
night light

TYPICAL VISITORS
sparrows and towhees
starlings and blackbirds
thrashers and catbirds
redpolls and siskins
robins and thrushes

3 Push the narrow end of the cheese grater on to the post and secure it with nails through the holes left by the handle rivets.

Above: *Blackbirds* (Turdus merula) *are among the most frequent visitors to birdbaths, splashing to wet their feathers.*

4 Squeeze the two sides of the lid handle together to insert them into the wide end of the grater. Place a night light inside the grater. This can then be lit to provide an interesting garden feature and prevent the water from freezing on cold days.

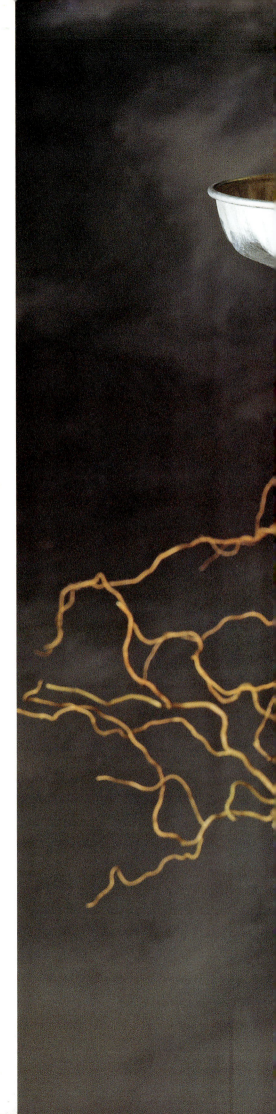

BOXES AND ROOSTS

Perhaps it is the opportunity to create a world in miniature, while simultaneously giving nature a helping hand, that has ensured the continued popularity of nest-box construction. Bird boxes and roosts can be plain, pretty or fanciful without affecting their primary function. Having satisfied the basic requirements, the finish is up to the individual. The projects in the following pages present a wide variety of ways to provide your local feathered community with nesting and sheltering sites.

Left: *Although highly embellished, this house still retains its practical function, providing a safe, dry site for birds to nest.*

Above: *Simple, home-made nest boxes make charming decorative features that enhance many different garden settings.*

Above: *An enclosed box with a round hole attracts small birds. It should be positioned high up in a tree, away from predators.*

Above: *A pretty dovecote provides pigeons and doves with a stylish place to shelter from wind and rain, and to roost overnight.*

ENCLOSED NEST BOX

This box will attract small birds to your garden. The round entrance hole is designed to suit species such as tits and titmice. Once birds have taken up residence, they could return year after year.

1 The wood used in nest boxes should preferably be hardwood, such as oak. Softer woods such as pine can also be used, but will start to rot more quickly. Whatever wood you use will last longer if you give the finished box a coat of exterior-grade varnish.

2 Measure the dimensions on the wood, referring to the template at the back of the book, and mark them clearly using a pencil and carpenter's square. Always double-check your measurements before cutting. Mark the names of each section in pencil.

3 Cut the pieces using a sharp carpentry saw and put them to one side. Sand off any splintered edges to the wood.

4 Carefully screw the sections together. Don't use nails as these can cause the wood to split, allowing water into the box.

5 On the front face of the box, make a hole with a large drill bit. Attach the roof, using the rubber strip as a hinge. Varnish and fix the bird box in the garden, choosing a suitable spot out of direct sun and high enough to be out of reach of predators.

YOU WILL NEED
length of wood, 142 x 15 x 1cm/ 56¾ x 6 x ½in
pencil
ruler
carpenter's square
saw
sandpaper
screws
screwdriver
drill with 3cm/1¼in drill bit
rubber strip (for hinge)
varnish
paintbrush

TYPICAL INHABITANTS
tits and titmice
wrens
house sparrows
nuthatches
house finches

OPEN-FRONTED NEST BOX

Not all of the birds that may nest in your garden like boxes with small entrance holes. Open-fronted boxes are designed to suit robins, wrens, spotted flycatchers and pied wagtails, and if you made the dimensions bigger, you could attract blackbirds and maybe even kestrels.

Above: *A nest box with a large, square entrance hole as shown in this project will attract robins and wrens. However, spotted flycatchers* (Muscicipa striata) *(above) will nest in a similar box with an entirely open front. This species begins nesting later than many other garden birds, using twigs, grass and moss bound with cobwebs to make the basic structure. The nest is then lined with feathers. An entirely open-faced box could also attract pied wagtails, American robins, phoebes, blue jays and some sparrows and swallows.*

YOU WILL NEED

length of wood 15mm/⅝in thick
wood glue
hammer
nails or panel pins, pencil
strip of sacking or rubber
   (for hinge)
varnish, paintbrush

TYPICAL INHABITANTS

robins and wrens
spotted flycatchers, pied wagtails,
   American robins, phoebes, blue
   jays and some sparrows and
   swallows – will nest in a similar
   box with an entirely open front

1 Cut out the wood using the template given in the back of the book. Arrange the pieces in position to make sure that they all fit properly.

2 Glue the low front of the box to the base. Give the glue a little time to dry. Now add one of the side pieces of your nest box. Glue it in place carefully.

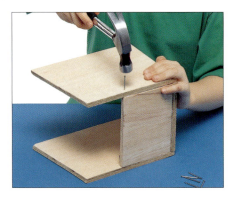

3 Glue on the other side and nail all the pieces together. Position the box on the rear board, and draw round it in pencil.

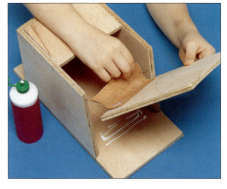

4 Using your pencil guidelines, nail the rear to the box. Add the roof by gluing and nailing on the sacking hinge.

5 Your nest box will last longer if you give it a coat of exterior-grade varnish both inside and out. Leave the box overnight to let the varnish dry completely.

6 Nail your box to a tree, shed or post, about 2m/7ft from the ground. Face the box away from any direct sunlight, as this may harm very young birds.

CUSTOMIZED NEST BOX

Ready-made nest boxes are available in every shape and size. An inexpensive birdhouse can be transformed with a splash of paint and a few decorative touches. The Shaker-style paintwork on this birdhouse uses leftover paint, the finial is cut from scrap wood and the perch is an apple-tree twig.

Above: *Studies have shown that tits (Paridae) are opportunistic birds, quickly able to adjust to new situations and turn them to their advantage. Members of this family are the species most likely to nest in an enclosed nest box such as this one. To ensure that the nest box gives you maximum pleasure, position it so it can be seen from the house.*

YOU WILL NEED

nest box
emulsion (latex) paint in 2 colours
paintbrush
permanent marker (felt-tip) pen
decorative finial cut from a piece
    of scrap pine
PVA (white) glue
drill
apple-tree twig

TYPICAL INHABITANTS

tits, titmice and chickadees
house sparrows
nuthatches and crested flycatchers
woodpeckers
jackdaws and pigeons – will nest in
    a larger box of this type

1 Paint the box with the first colour of emulsion paint and set it aside to dry. Draw the door and heart motifs using the permanent marker pen.

2 Fill in the design and the finial with the second colour of emulsion paint and leave to dry completely. Glue the finial at the front of the roof ridge using PVA glue.

3 Drill a hole of the same diameter as the apple-tree twig beneath the entrance hole. Apply a little glue to the twig and push it in position. Allow the glue to dry.

DECORATED BIRDHOUSES

Inexpensive ready-made plain boxes can be customized to suit your taste. Paint makes for the simplest transformations – an alpine chalet and a Shaker-style dwelling are pictured here. You could also create a leafy hideaway using fabric shapes. Paint each house with primer before you begin, and allow to dry.

YOU WILL NEED
ready-made birdhouses
paintbrushes
emulsion (latex) paints
matt varnish and brush
pencil, paper and scissors
self-adhesive roof flashing
waterproof green canvas
staple gun
waterproofing wax (optional)

TYPICAL INHABITANTS
tits, titmice and chickadees

1 To create an alpine chalet, draw the design on the box. Paint the roof, shutters and other details in blue. When this is dry, paint the walls of the house in rust red.

2 Add details on the gable, shutters and stonework in white and grey. Paint flowers, grass and leaves along the front and sides in yellow and green. Varnish when dry.

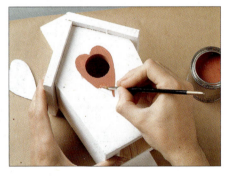

1 To make a Shaker-style dwelling, cut a heart out of paper and position it over the entry hole. Draw around it in pencil and paint the heart rust red.

2 Paint the walls in duck-egg blue using a larger paintbrush. When this layer is dry, paint on little starbursts in rust red using a very fine artist's brush.

3 Cut a piece of roof flashing to fit the birdhouse roof. Cover the roof, folding the edges under the eaves. Protect the paintwork with matt varnish.

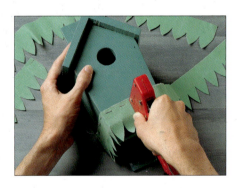

1 To make a leafy hideaway, paint the birdhouse a colour complementary to your green canvas, such as mid-blue, and leave to dry. Cut the canvas into 4cm/1½in bands and scallop one edge. Staple the bands on to the house, starting at the base and allowing the scallops to overhang.

2 Staple more canvas bands around the front and sides, with each layer overlapping the last. When you reach the entry hole, snip the top of the canvas and glue it down inside. Staple on the next band, then trim back the central scallop to form a few small fronds above the entry hole.

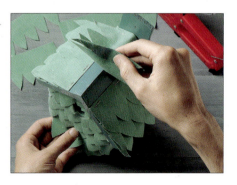

3 Overlay strips on the side of the roof. Cut the top strip double the width, with a scalloped edge along both sides, so that it fits over the roof ridge. Finally, staple bands along the gable ends. Spray the finished house with waterproofing wax, if not using a waterproof fabric.

LAVENDER HIDEAWAY

This hand-painted project takes only a short time to make using a ready-made birdhouse. Even the heaviest shower pours freely off the lead roof, leaving the occupants warm and dry inside.

1 Paint the birdhouse with lilac emulsion and allow it to dry. Sketch out the decorative design using a pencil. Fill in the sketch using acrylic or watercolour paints. When dry, cover the whole house with several coats of exterior-grade matt varnish.

2 Make a paper pattern to fit the roof, using the template at the back of the book as a guide. Allow 12mm/½in extra for turning under each side and the rear, and 32mm/1¼in extra for the scallops.

YOU WILL NEED

wooden birdhouse
lilac emulsion (latex) paint
medium and fine paintbrushes
pencil
acrylic or watercolour paints
exterior-grade varnish
paper
scissors
thin sheet lead
tin snips or craft knife
soft hammer or wooden mallet

TYPICAL INHABITANTS

tits, titmice and chickadees
wrens and nuthatches
bluebirds and house sparrows

3 Transfer the design on to a piece of thin sheet lead and cut it out using tin snips or a craft knife. Wear protective gloves or wash your hands thoroughly afterward.

4 Hold the lead roof in place and mould to shape by tapping the lead with a soft hammer or wooden mallet until the correct fit is achieved. Turn the 12mm/½in allowance under at the back and at the eaves to secure the roof in place.

Above: Hole-nesters such as nuthatches (Sitta europaea) are well suited to this box.

FOLK-ART BOX

This box is simple to make, but with its traditional weathered look, it makes the perfect springtime retreat for tits, titmice, chickadees and other hole-nesters, such as nuthatches and house sparrows. Mounted on a post in a quiet spot, it should be safe from prowling predators such as cats.

1 Mark and cut the basic house on MDF or plywood following the template at the back. Mark a vertical line on the front panel. Mark a horizontal line across at the base of the triangle. Where the two lines cross, draw a 32mm/1¼in circle using compasses. Cut out the hole by first drilling a pilot hole, then enlarging it with a padsaw. Assemble the front, back, sides, base and the smaller roof piece of the hut using PVA glue and panel pins hammered down flush with the surface of the wood.

2 Paint the whole house, including the loose roof piece, with blue-grey emulsion paint. When dry, paint the walls of the house white. When these are dry (about 2–3 hours), distress the surfaces by rubbing with medium-grade sandpaper until the undercoat shows through.

3 Wearing protective gloves, cut a strip of lead the depth of the roof by 50mm/2in using tin snips. Staple this to the loose roof half. Position the roof halves together, bend the lead to fit and staple through the lead into the fixed roof half.

4 Drill two small holes just below and to either side of the entrance hole. Bend a piece of copper wire into a flattened loop slightly wider than the distance between the holes. Pass the two ends of the wire through the holes and turn them down just inside the box to hold the perch in place.

Above: *Titmice (Paridae) nest in tree holes and bird boxes. They line their nests with warm materials, such as moss and leaves.*

Above: *This box can be adapted with different embellishments. It can be fixed on a pole or hung from a tree.*

ROCK-A-BYE BIRDIE BOX

This box constructed from plywood is made to suit small, acrobatic birds such as wrens, nuthatches, tits and titmice. The removable roof is covered with flashing to repel rainwater. The box hangs on stout string, though if you have a problem with predators, it would be safer to use greased wire.

Above: *The small size of the wren means that it is often overlooked, but its acrobatic skills make it ideally suited to this box.*

YOU WILL NEED
paper
pencil
scissors
6mm/¼in plywood
drill
sandpaper
fretsaw
V-board (birdsmouth board or clamp)
18 x 6mm/¾ x ¼in D-shaped
    moulding
tenon saw
wood glue
nails
hammer
scrap wood
varnish
paintbrush
self-adhesive roof flashing
knife
cutting mat
string or wire

TYPICAL INHABITANTS
tits, titmice and chickadees
wrens

1 Copy the templates at the back of the book, cut out and use to mark out the shapes for the base and roof on thin plywood. Drill an entry hole in one side of the top and sand the edges.

2 Cut out the plywood shapes using a fretsaw and V-board. Next, cut the D-shaped moulding into 10cm/4in lengths to make the base and 15cm/6in lengths to make the roof.

3 Glue and then nail the lengths of moulding around the base, with the flat side facing outward. You'll find the easiest way of working is to start with the central strip and then work out.

4 Make a simple template to the width of the box from a piece of scrap wood and use it to space the sides of the roof. Attach the roof slats as before, allowing for an overlap on each side.

5 Mark a line around the base, about 6mm/¼in below the top edge of the sides, and trim back the mouldings to this level to allow the roof to overlap the base. Apply a coat of varnish to the box.

6 Cut a strip of 15cm/6in-wide roof flashing, long enough to cover the roof, and smooth it over the moulding strips. Hammer the surface if you wish. Attach a length of string for hanging.

SLATE-ROOFED COTTAGE

As long as a birdhouse is weatherproof and sited in a safe, sheltered position, its external appearance will not affect the inhabitants. This sturdy-looking house, which will suit sparrows, is actually made of wood faced with self-hardening clay and roofed with slate.

Above: *As its name suggests, the house sparrow usually nests near buildings. It is well adapted to living alongside humans.*

YOU WILL NEED
pencil
ruler
2cm/¾in pine board
tenon saw
drill
wood glue
nails, hammer
enamel paints
paintbrushes
paper
scissors
terracotta self-hardening clay
board
rolling pin
knife
epoxy resin glue
blunt-ended modelling tool
acrylic paints
satin exterior varnish
varnish brush
slate
face mask
hacksaw

TYPICAL INHABITANTS
sparrows and house finches
tits, titmice and chickadees

1 Using the templates at the back of the book, cut out the birdhouse pieces from the board. Drill an entry hole in one side only. Glue and nail the box together. Draw, then paint, the door and window on the front.

3 Cover the whole of the front of the house with a layer of epoxy resin glue, but take care to avoid the painted door and window. Now carefully lay the clay over the front. You may need to adjust it slightly to fit it in the exact position.

5 Paint over some of the bricks using acrylic paints to imitate the varied colours of real brickwork. Leave it to dry, and then coat with a satin exterior varnish.

2 Make paper patterns of the sides and front. Cut out the entry hole, front door and window. Roll out the clay to a depth of 8mm/⅜in thick. Lay the patterns on the clay and cut around them.

4 Inscribe the fancy brickwork around the window and door using a blunt-ended modelling tool, then use a ruler to press in horizontal lines as a guide for the standard brickwork. Inscribe the brickwork with the modelling tool. Repeat on the side walls.

6 Cut a piece of slate to size, wearing a face mask. It helps to saw through each side edge before cutting across. Drill four holes for nails and nail the roof to the sides.

RIDGE TILE RETREAT

This elegant birdhouse is divided into two. With an entry hole at each end, it suits larger birds, such as starlings and purple martins, which live in colonies. An old ridge tile makes an excellent roof.

1 Using the templates at the back of the book, mark and cut out the components for the birdhouse, adapting the pitch of the roof to fit your tile. Drill an entry hole in each end.

2 Sand all the surfaces. Now glue and then nail the floor to the sides. Next measure and mark the centre line of the box and glue the dividing wall in position.

3 Glue and nail each gable end piece to the sides. Paint the outside of the birdhouse and leave it to dry thoroughly.

4 Place the ridge tile in position on top of the birdhouse. This house can be erected on a post or simply placed at medium height in a quiet location.

Below: *Starlings* (Sturnus vulgaris) *are gregarious birds that feed and roost in flocks. This box will suit two pairs of birds.*

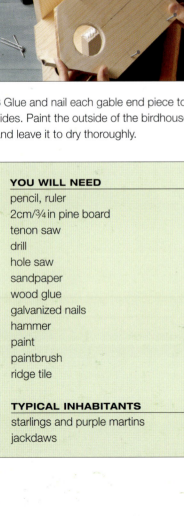

YOU WILL NEED

pencil, ruler
2cm/¾in pine board
tenon saw
drill
hole saw
sandpaper
wood glue
galvanized nails
hammer
paint
paintbrush
ridge tile

TYPICAL INHABITANTS

starlings and purple martins
jackdaws

SWIFT NURSERY

Swifts build their nests in wall crevices, tall chimneys, under the eaves of houses, in hollow trees or in tunnel-shaped boxes. Although they will sometimes take to boxes with front-facing access holes, an entrance hole underneath is better, as it prevents house sparrows and starlings taking over the box.

Above: *Swifts* (Apus apus) *spend almost their entire lives on the wing, but touch down to nest, often high up on walls.*

1 Using the templates at the back of the book, mark and cut out all the pieces for the box, except the front, from pine board. Cut lengths of batten for the front. Cut a paper pattern for the entry hole at one end of the base and cut it out using a fretsaw.

2 Glue and nail the base to the back of the box. Glue and nail the ends in place and add the top batten. Cut the tongue-and-groove board into 15cm/6in lengths. Glue and nail to the front of the box, attaching it to the batten and the edge of the base.

YOU WILL NEED

pencil, ruler
carpenter's square
2cm/¾in pine board
tenon saw
2cm/¾in square pine batten
paper
fretsaw
V-board (birdsmouth board or clamp)
hammer
nails
wood glue
tongue-and-groove board
drill
sandpaper
emulsion (latex) paint in cream
    and black
varnish
paintbrushes
self-adhesive roof flashing
scissors

TYPICAL INHABITANTS
swifts

3 Allow the glue time to dry. Then drill a 15mm/⅝in hole at each joint, placing a piece of scrap wood behind the tongue-and-groove to prevent it splitting. Now trim the lower edge of each board to form a chevron shape. Drill two holes in the back of the box for fixing to a wall. Sand and paint the box, then leave to dry. Paint the outside with varnish to protect the wood.

4 Cut two battens for the roof, using the template at the back. Mark positions for the battens on the underside of the roof using the box as a guide. Fix the battens with short nails. Paint the underside black. Cover the top of the roof with strips of self-adhesive flashing and fit the roof on to the box. Overlap the last strip of flashing to the back of the box. Fix the box on to a wall.

POST BOX

Thick wooden stakes can be hollowed out and turned into unusual nest boxes for small birds such as tits, titmice and nuthatches. The boxes can be sited on their own or form part of a garden fence. The cover of roof flashing protects the box from the elements and also helps prevent the wood from splitting.

Above: *White-breasted nuthatches (Sitta carolinensis)* build their nests in tree cavities and in birdhouses. The nest, usually made of twigs and grass, is lined with hair and feathers. In winter, they commonly visit backyard bird tables to take peanut picks, sunflowers, suet, and mixed seeds.

1 Using a 25mm/1in bit, drill an entry hole into the side of the post 5cm/2in from the end, then drill out the end to a depth of about 15cm/6in.

2 Use a chisel and mallet to remove the waste wood left in the end of the post after drilling. Work to create a roughly circular cavity at least 15cm/6in deep.

3 Cover the end of the post with self-adhesive roof flashing. Pierce the flashing in the centre of the entry hole and cut back to the edges. Now turn back the flashing inside the hole, but take care not to significantly reduce the size of the entry hole which the birds will use.

4 Wearing protective gloves, cut out a circle of lead flashing for the lid and remove one quarter of the circle, using the template at the back of the book. Clamp the lead between two pieces of scrap wood and fold one cut edge at 90 degrees. Fold the second edge over twice at 90 degrees, as shown.

5 Wearing gloves, bend the lead to a cone shape. Then join the seam by squeezing the edges together with pliers. Flatten the seam against the cone.

6 Attach the roof to the post using two nails, but leave one not fully nailed in so that it can be removed to give access to the box when you need to clean it out.

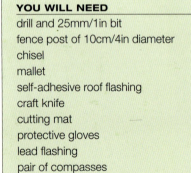

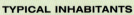

YOU WILL NEED
drill and 25mm/1in bit
fence post of 10cm/4in diameter
chisel
mallet
self-adhesive roof flashing
craft knife
cutting mat
protective gloves
lead flashing
pair of compasses
pencil
ruler
scrap wood
vice
pliers
nails
hammer

TYPICAL INHABITANTS
tits, titmice and chickadees
wrens
nuthatches

CLAY POT ROOST

For this project you will need access to a kiln (perhaps through a local education centre or school), but you do not need to be skilled in pottery. Cut the entry hole to suit your choice of potential resident, and site the pot in a sheltered position, out of reach of predators.

Above: *The domestic pigeon (Columba livia) is a common sight in towns and gardens in many parts of the world. This species may shelter or nest in the pot roost if you make the dimensions and entry hole a little bigger. The dimensions given here will provide a roost for wrens, tits, titmice, nuthatches and house sparrows.*

YOU WILL NEED
paper
pencil
scissors
latex gloves
clay
rolling pin
craft knife
length of 10cm/4in diameter plastic
    plumbing pipe
round cutter
bradawl or awl
fresh leaves, to decorate
kiln

TYPICAL INHABITANTS
wrens
tits, titmice and chickadees
nuthatches
house sparrows
street pigeons and starlings
crested flycatchers

1 From the paper, cut a circle 12cm/4½in across, a rectangle 12 x 17cm/4½ x 6½in, and a semicircle 38cm/15in across. Roll out the clay to 8mm/⅜in thickness and cut out the shapes. Cover the pipe in paper and roll the rectangle of clay around it.

3 Keeping the pipe inside the clay cylinder, add the circular base, smoothing the edges together. Press fresh leaves into the cylinder to decorate. Remove the pipe.

5 Mould a small bird from leftover clay to decorate the top of the lid. Model the wings separately and then moisten them before pressing them on to the body. Draw the feathers and eyes using a bradawl or awl.

2 Seal the joint at the side by wetting the overlap slightly and then smoothing it down with your thumb. Now cut an entry hole 25mm/1in in diameter, positioned about a third of the way down from the top, using a plain round cutter.

4 To make the lid of the roost, curl the semicircle of clay into a cone shape. Join the edges as before by moistening and then smoothing them with your fingers.

6 Attach the bird by smoothing a little clay over the base of the bird and the top of the lid. Wrap in plastic and allow to dry slowly. When completely dry, fire the base and the lid separately in a kiln.

SEASIDE NEST BOX

Inspired by early twentieth-century seaside architecture, this pretty box is designed for hole-nesters such as tits and nuthatches. Fretwork is satisfying to make, but it does require practice and patience. However, your efforts will be rewarded once you see your creation hanging on the garden wall.

Above: *Position the box high in a tree if you want to provide a nest site for birds such as the tufted titmouse (Baeolophus bicolor).*

1 Using the templates at the back of the book, mark and cut out the base, back, sides and lid from 2cm/¾in pine. Cut the notches in the side pieces. Plane the edges of the base and lid to line up with the sides. Cut a length of dowelling for the perch.

2 Mark out the back plate, front, circular frame for the entry hole and the decorative panel for the lid front on 4mm/⅙in plywood and cut out using a fretsaw and V-board. Cut out a 2.5cm/1in entry hole in the front panel. Sand all the surfaces.

YOU WILL NEED
ruler, pencil
jigsaw
2cm/¾in pine board
tenon saw
plane
8mm/⅜in dowelling
4mm/⅙in plywood
fretsaw
V-board (birdsmouth board or clamp)
drill
sandpaper
wood glue
plated moulding pins
hammer, nails
watercolour paints in cobalt blue,
    burnt umber, turquoise, yellow
    ochre, burnt sienna
paintbrushes
petroleum jelly
2 butterfly hinges, with screws
tourmaline antiquing medium
white emulsion (latex) paint
blowtorch
satin yacht varnish
screwdriver and screws

TYPICAL INHABITANTS
tits, titmice and nuthatches
bluebirds
tree swallows

3 Glue the sides, base and back support together and secure with moulding pins. Glue and nail the fretwork panel to the front edge of the lid. Drill a hole for the perch below the entry hole, and glue into place, then glue and nail the front to the sides.

4 Paint the box with a dilute mixture of cobalt blue and burnt umber watercolour paints, in equal proportions. Leave to dry, then smear on a thin layer of petroleum jelly with your fingers. To age the hinges, paint with tourmaline antiquing medium.

5 Treating one surface at a time, apply a coat of white emulsion paint and dry it with a blowtorch to make the paint crack. Add a little turquoise and yellow ochre watercolour to the emulsion to make green for the entry hole frame and backboard.

6 Glue and nail the back panel on to the box. To age the paintwork, apply a dilute mixture of yellow ochre and burnt sienna watercolour until you achieve the desired effect. Leave to dry, then finish with varnish. Screw on the hinges to attach the lid.

DUCK HOUSE

You don't need a very large pond to provide a home for ducks such as mallards. If possible, the house should be positioned on an island or raft to provide protection from predators. The ramp for this desirable house has horizontal struts to make sure the occupants don't slip. Post caps on each leg will protect the wood on dry land. If it is to stand in water, use wood pressure-treated with preservative.

YOU WILL NEED

2cm/¾in pine board
45mm/1¾in square pine batten
   (strip)
20 x 45mm/¾ x 1¾in pine batten
   (strip)
rebated ship-lap boards
pencil
ruler
carpenter's square
tenon saw
jigsaw
sandpaper, wood glue
nails, hammer
exterior paint
paintbrush
corrugated roofing sheet
polystyrene (Styrofoam) filler
roofing screws and cups
screwdriver
wood decking or treated wood
flat work surface

TYPICAL INHABITANTS

ducks, including mallards and
   shovellers

Left: *The mallard (Anas platyrhynchos) is one of the most widespread and familiar ducks in the world. These waterbirds sometimes nest in gardens near lakes or rivers, where there is thick vegetation to provide cover for the nest site. The appearance of the male differs quite markedly through the year. In the breeding season the handsome green head, white collar and brown chest distinguish him from the female. In late summer he moults into eclipse plumage, which quite closely resembles the female's in its drab hues.*

Left: *Shovellers (Anas clypeata) have a broad bill that enables these waterfowl to feed more easily in shallow water. They typically swim with their bill open, trailing through the water to catch invertebrates, although they also forage both by up-ending themselves and catching insects on reeds. These ducks choose wet ground, often some distance from open water, as a nesting site. Like the young of other waterfowl, the young birds take to the water soon after hatching.*

1 Mark out and cut out all the components for the duck house using the templates given at the back of the book. Carefully cut out the curved roof battens and then the arched opening using a jigsaw. Sand all the edges.

2 On a large, flat work surface, lay out two of the legs parallel to one another. Position the cross rail on top of the legs, using the carpenter's square to make sure all three parts are at right angles to one another. Now attach the cross rail using wood glue and nails.

3 Turn the leg assembly over and attach the first curved roof batten. Repeat the process with the other two legs.

4 Connect the front and back with the two lower cross rails. These are nailed to the inner side of the legs.

5 Nail and glue the upper side rails at both sides. These rails are attached to the outside of the legs. This completes the basic framework of the house.

6 Ship-lap the back and sides of the house, starting at the top. Glue and nail the top piece in place, but don't drive the nails in fully. Only do so after the lower piece has been glued and nailed in place.

7 Ship-lap the front in the same way, securing the door sides first. Make sure that you align the door sides carefully to give a straight, clean line when the duck house is assembled.

8 Finish off the house walls by attaching the four corner pieces. Paint the house inside and out, and allow it to dry. Put in the floor, which rests in place on the cross rails.

▶

9 Cut a piece of roofing sheet to the measurements given at the back of the book, and cut two strips of polystyrene filler to fit the arched front and back walls. Offer up the roof, locating it centrally.

10 Attach the roof to the front and back walls of the house, using special roofing screws and cups.

11 Make a simple ramp by joining two planks of wood decking with cross pieces. Nail an extra cross piece to the back of the ramp at the top to hook over the batten under the door.

RUSTIC CABIN

This charming cabin is constructed around a basic box with a sloping roof. Faced with 'logs', it will harmonize well with any garden setting, offering a nursery for hole-nesting birds.

YOU WILL NEED

6mm/¼in medium-density fibreboard (MDF) or exterior-grade plywood
ruler, pencil
hammer, nails
saw
twigs and branches
axe or small-scale log splitter
glue gun and glue sticks
dark grey emulsion (latex) paint
medium paintbrush
drill
padsaw (keyhole saw)
100 x 12mm/4 x ½in coach bolt
moss or moss-covered branch

TYPICAL INHABITANTS

sparrows and wrens
tits, titmice and chickadees

1 Mark and cut out the basic house in MDF or plywood following the template at the back of the book. Make 'logs' from small branches by splitting the branches lengthways so there is a flat side for sticking to the box and a rounded surface with bark for the outside.

2 Assemble the basic box with glue and nails. Paint it with dark grey emulsion paint so that any small gaps between the logs will not show when they are attached.

3 Glue the logs to the front. To make the entry hole, cut through the logs and the box below using a drill and then a padsaw.

4 Cut a 12mm/½in hole and insert a coach bolt for the 'chimney'. Continue to fix logs to the rest of the house, shaping them to fit and making the roof logs overlap the walls slightly as an added protection against rain. Neaten the corners of the walls by trimming the individual log ends with a saw. Glue a piece of moss or moss-covered branch to the opening as a perch.

Left: *Tits, titmice and chickadees – such as this Carolina chickadee (Parus carolinensis) – like to nest in tree stumps or birdhouses. Place the finished log cabin high in a tree to attract hole-nesting species.*

LOG CABIN

Designed for wrens, which like open-fronted nest boxes, this log cabin-effect box will blend in well with the natural environment. Position it low down in a well-hidden site, preferably surrounded by thorny shrubbery, and well away from any other birdhouses.

Above: *Winter wrens (Troglodytes troglodytes) are easily overlooked because of their tiny size and skulking habits. However, their song is surprisingly loud. These little birds breed from March to July, constructing a domed structure in thick vegetation, where the female lays 5–8 eggs. The young hatch after 16–17 days and take a similar time to fledge.*

YOU WILL NEED
sticks – newly-cut hazelwood from
   coppiced woodland is best, as
   the coppiced stems can be cut to
   length to produce short, strong,
   straight sticks
ruler
pencil
tenon saw
bench hook
hammer
short, fine nails or sturdy panel pins
10cm/4in square plastic tray
piece of turf
knife

TYPICAL INHABITANTS
wrens
swallows and sparrows – may use
   this box as a roost

1 Select evenly sized, straight sticks and cut them to length, using a tenon saw and bench hook. You will need 4 sturdy uprights 15cm/6in long, 10 sticks to make the base 12cm/4¾in long, and about 50 sticks for the sides, 10cm/4in long.

3 Attach the two sides by nailing more small sticks across the back. You may need to brace the structure. Work from bottom to top, hammering nails into the uprights at an angle, to keep the structure strong.

5 Build up the top of the box by adding two more of the shorter sticks to each side, on top of the existing pieces. Gently nail the new sticks on top of the walls.

2 Construct the first side by nailing 10cm/4in lengths to two of the uprights. Use short, fine nails or sturdy panel pins. Nail on the two end sticks first to make a rectangle, then fill in with other sticks. Repeat to make the other side.

4 Turn the box over. Attach one stick at the top of the front, then leave a gap of about 5cm/2in for the entrance hole before completing the rest of the front. Use the 12cm/4¾in sticks to make the base.

6 Fit the tray into the top so that it rests on the uprights, or so that the lip rests on top of the walls. Cut a piece of turf to fit and place it in the tray to make the roof.

THATCHED BIRDHOUSE

As long as the basic box requirements are fulfilled, the finish is up to you. Tailor-made for hole-nesters such as sparrows, bluebirds, swallows and titmice, this box should be sited somewhere quiet so that the birds are not disturbed while nesting. Leave the house out during winter for use as a snug roost.

Above: *Eastern bluebirds benefit from the provision of nest boxes because starlings and sparrows can take over their nest sites.*

YOU WILL NEED

pencil, ruler
carpenter's square
6mm/¼in medium density fibreboard
   (MDF)
tenon saw
drill
wood glue
masking tape
small metal eyelet and hook
craft knife
cutting mat
metal ruler
self-adhesive roof flashing
ready-mixed tile cement
palette knife
aquarium gravel
sisal hanging-basket liner
PVA (white) glue
paintbrush
raffia
large-eyed needle
clothes pegs
diluted brown watercolour paint
matt varnish
varnish brush

TYPICAL INHABITANTS

sparrows, bluebirds and swallows
tits, titmice and chickadees

1 Following the templates at the back of the book, mark and cut out the component parts from MDF. Drill an entry hole in the front wall and, if required, drill a small hole in the back wall for hanging.

2 Glue the base and walls together and then hold the structure in position with masking tape until the glue is quite dry. Screw in an eyelet 1cm/½in from the top back corner of the right-hand wall.

3 Cut a strip of roof flashing 13cm/5in wide to the length of the roof ridge. Position the two roof pieces side by side, leaving enough of a gap to allow the roof to hinge open. Remove the backing and cover the ridge with the flashing.

4 Working on a small area at a time, spread ready-mixed tile cement over the house walls. Embed aquarium gravel firmly into the cement, choosing darker stones to outline the entry hole. Cover the walls of the house completely.

5 Coat the sisal with diluted PVA glue and leave to dry. Cut a rectangle 28 x 14cm/ 11 x 5½in for the thatch and a strip 15 x 7.5cm/6 x 3in for the ridge. Stitch two rows of large cross-stitch in raffia along the sides of this strip, then glue and stitch it across the thatch.

6 Glue the thatch to the roof. Secure it with clothes pegs until dry. Screw in the hook at the back of the roof, then glue the other side of the roof to the walls, securing it with masking tape until quite dry. Wash the cement with brown watercolour and, when dry, give it a coat of varnish.

NESTY NOOK

This cosy home to suit hole-nesters, such as wrens and nuthatches, is formed from plastic-coated chicken wire covered with moss. To suit wrens, place the nest in a hidden position, low down in thick undergrowth. To suit nuthatches, the nest should be placed in a tree.

Above: *Red-breasted nuthatches (Sitta canadensis)* usually nest in cavities in pine trees. They smear the nest entrance with pitch to discourage predators. The female lays 5–6 eggs inside. In winter, the birds forage widely. They feed mainly on pine seeds, but will also visit bird tables to take suet and seeds. In summer, their diet includes insects and wood-boring grubs.

YOU WILL NEED
chicken wire
wire cutters
large leaves
sisal hanging-basket liner
scissors
pliers
hair net
moss
sea grass string
garden wire

TYPICAL INHABITANTS
wrens
nuthatches
tits, titmice and chickadees
sparrows
woodpeckers and jackdaws –
    will use a nest with slightly larger
    dimensions, placed high in a tree

1 Cut a square of chicken wire measuring about 30cm/12in. Line it with large leaves. Cut a square of hanging basket liner made of sisal to the same size and lay it down on top of the leaves.

2 Fold the four corners into the centre and join the sides by twisting the ends of the wires together. Leave the centre open. Tuck in the wire ends to ensure that there are no sharp bits poking out to harm the bird.

3 Pull at the wire structure from the front and back to 'puff' it out and create a larger space inside for the bird to nest.

4 Carefully stretch a hair net over the whole nest structure. Take care to keep the entrance hole clear.

5 Stuff moss evenly between the nest and the hair net to cover the chicken wire completely. Work on one part at a time until you are satisfied with the look of the whole.

6 To define the entry hole, form a ring of sea grass string and secure it by twisting garden wire around it. Wire it into position around the hole.

SCALLOP SHELTER

This little nest designed for swallows and martins is made of papier-mâché. It is easily replaced each season, though the chicken wire container will last longer. Attach it to the wall with two cup hooks, in a dry place under the eaves. The scallop shell is purely decorative.

Above: *Barn swallows* (Hirundo rustica) *originally nested on rocky ledges, but now they mostly nest under the eaves of buildings, using mud for the nest itself. They are found in most parts of the world.*

YOU WILL NEED

newspaper
bowl of water
plastic bowl
wallpaper paste
brush
scissors
corrugated cardboard
pencil
masking tape
acrylic paints
paintbrush
chicken wire
protective gloves
wire cutters
small pliers
drill
scallop shell
florist's wire

TYPICAL INHABITANTS

swallows
martins
tits and titmice

1 To make the papier-mâché, tear a newspaper into small squares and soak it in water. Cover one half of a plastic bowl with a layer of wet, unpasted pieces of paper. The pieces should slightly overlap.

2 Brush paste liberally over the first layer and add more pieces, pasting each layer, until you have built up about six layers. Leave it to dry out in a warm place such as an airing cupboard.

3 When the papier-mâché is completely dry, remove it from the plastic bowl and trim the rough edges to make a neat half-bowl shape. Now cut out a semicircle of corrugated cardboard, which will form the backing for the nest.

4 Attach the cardboard to the papier-mâché bowl shape using masking tape, then reinforce the structure by adding a few layers of pasted paper over the back and edges. Leave the nest in a warm place to dry out thoroughly.

5 Paint the nest in variegated muddy tones. Cut a piece of chicken wire using wire cutters. Wrap it around the nest and join the wire ends together at the sides.

6 Squeeze the chicken wire with the pliers to shape it to the form. Drill two small holes in the top of the scallop shell and one at the bottom, and wire it on to the frame.

WILLOW STICK NEST

Half coconuts are just the right shape and size to make snug nests for small birds. Two halves are wedged into a bunch of withes, and a woven sea grass wall completes the nest.

1 Soak the withes overnight to make them pliable. Wedge them around a stick using a napkin ring. Saw a coconut in half and scrape out the contents. Using raffia, tie the withes together at the top.

2 Insert the coconut halves. Starting by the rim of the lower half, weave sea grass string around the withes for three rounds.

3 Create a gap by doubling the string back on itself and changing the direction of the weaving for about four rounds.

4 Complete the weaving with three more rounds. Wedge the top of the coconut into position above the weaving and secure it by re-tying the withes at the top if necessary.

Left: *Acrobatic black-capped chickadees* (Parus atricapillus) *construct cup-shaped nests of plant fibres, moss, fur and feathers. They also use artificial nests, such as these.*

YOU WILL NEED

about 15 withes (willow sticks)
straight stick or bamboo pole
wooden napkin ring
coconut
saw
knife
raffia
sea grass string
scissors

TYPICAL INHABITANTS

wrens
tits, titmice and chickadees

HOLLOW LOG NEST BOX

Choose an appealing log for this nest box. Depending on its size, you can adapt it to suit the type of bird you want to attract, from tits and titmice to woodpeckers. Mossy logs look beautiful, as do chunks of silver birch. Avoid pieces of wood with knots or branches, as they are difficult to split neatly.

Above: *Place the nest box high in a tree to attract woodpeckers, such as this great spotted (Dendrocopos major). These birds use their short, stiff tails to balance upright on the trunk while they extract grubs from beneath the bark. They usually nest in tree holes excavated with their sharp beaks.*

YOU WILL NEED
2 logs
pencil
ruler
straight-edged chisel
mallet
drill
saw
hammer
nails
garden wire
scissors
pliers

TYPICAL INHABITANTS
woodpeckers
tits, titmice and wrens
starlings

1 Mark out a square on the end of one log. Use a mallet and straight-edged chisel to split off the first side, making sure that you work evenly along the line.

3 Saw a 20mm/¾in slice off one end of the centre of the log to form the base.

5 Wrap a length of garden wire around the top of the box, twist the ends to tighten it and hold the sides securely together.

2 Repeat this process to remove all four sides of the square. Drill an entrance hole through one of the sides, making a sizeable hole if you want to attract woodpeckers.

4 Using the base piece, reassemble the log by nailing the four sides together.

6 Split the second log to make a roof for the nest box. Attach it using one long nail, so that the roof can easily swivel open.

NEST-IN-A-BOOT

An old boot provides the basis for this original nest box. It is half-filled with gravel to stabilize it, and a small basket makes a perfect foundation for the nest itself. Try to find an interesting seed pod or other natural decoration for the roof. The birds won't need the little ladder, but children will love it.

Above: *Blue tits and other members of the tit and titmouse family are the small birds most likely to use nest boxes. They construct a nest of moss, dry grass and twigs in a crevice or nest box.*

YOU WILL NEED
rubber boot
scissors
gravel
small round basket
bradawl or awl
string
small sticks
epoxy resin glue
wooden curtain ring
protective gloves
chicken wire
wire cutters
small pliers
sisal hanging-basket liner
large-eyed needle
raffia
interesting seed pod
garden wire

TYPICAL INHABITANTS
tits, titmice and chickadees
sparrows and wrens
starlings – may use this nest with
    a larger entry hole

1 Cut down the boot to a suitable size and cut out a small entry hole toward the top. Fill the bottom of the boot with gravel, then wedge a small round basket into position below the entry hole.

2 Make two small holes below the entry hole to either side. Thread a long piece of string through these and tie on little sticks to form a ladder. Glue on a wooden curtain ring over the entry hole as reinforcement.

3 To make the roof, cut a semicircular piece of chicken wire, using wire cutters and wearing protective gloves. Curve the wire to form a cone. Join the sides by twisting the ends of the wire together using pliers.

4 Wrap a piece of the sisal hanging-basket liner around the cone of chicken wire, pressing the wire rim firmly into the matting. Turn in the edges of both the matting and the chicken wire.

5 Sew cross-stitch along the join using string and a large-eyed needle. Now cross-stitch around the bottom with raffia. Insert the seed pod decoration into the point of the roof and glue in place.

6 Make four pairs of holes, evenly spaced around the rim of the boot. Attach the roof to the boot using four lengths of garden wire and twist the wires together. Snip off any excess wire.

DOVECOTE

This beautiful structure will make a comfortable roost for up to half a dozen doves, but it could be adapted to accommodate more birds by increasing the number of tiers. The dovecote is probably best sited on the side of a building, but it can also be mounted on a stout post.

Above: *Mourning doves (Zenaida macroura) live in both cities and rural areas, and will roost in tiered dovecotes. This structure is also suitable for pigeons.*

YOU WILL NEED
pencil
ruler
carpenter's square
12mm/½ in and 6mm/¼ in plywood
jigsaw
20mm/¾ in pine board
tenon saw
2 x 4.5cm/¾ x 1¾ in pine batten
  (strip)
sandpaper
wood glue
nails, hammer
drill
screws
screwdriver
paint
paintbrush
self-adhesive roof flashing
craft knife
cutting mat
metal ruler

TYPICAL INHABITANTS
doves and pigeons

1 Using the template at the back, mark and cut out the backboard from 12mm/½ in plywood with a jigsaw. Cut the roof shapes and front arches from 6mm/¼ in plywood.

3 Join the sides and centre by gluing and nailing on the front battens. Fit the back battens into the notches cut in the centre piece. Attach by nailing in the centre of the batten and at each end.

5 Cover the small roof sections with self-adhesive roof flashing. Cover the main roof with horizontal strips of flashing. Start from the bottom of the roof and overlap each section, allowing some overlap on the final piece to attach to the backboard.

2 Mark and cut out all the pine parts from 20mm/¾ in thick planks, following the templates provided. The sides and centre will require wide boards. Sand all surfaces.

4 Drill pilot holes for the screws in the backboard. Attach the backboard to the frame using glue and screws. Paint the frame and the arched fronts and leave to dry. Attach the fronts using glue and nails.

6 Using nails, assemble the last parts in the following order: first the small roof sections; then the floors; then the main roof. Attach the dovecote to a wall by screwing through the backboard from the inside. Take care when fixing, as the structure is heavy.

CLAPBOARD HOUSE

This smart New England-style house is suitable for hole-nesters such as sparrows and tree swallows. It will add a decorative feature to any garden, as well as providing small birds with a nesting site.

Above: *Tree sparrows build their nests from twigs and leaves lined with feathers, moss and hair. They nest either in natural cavities, such as holes in trees, cliffs or buildings, or use a nest box such as this one.*

YOU WILL NEED
6 mm/¼in medium-density
    fibreboard (MDF) or plywood
pencil, ruler
saw
PVA (white) glue
hammer, panel pins
birch veneer
coloured woodstain
scalpel or craft knife
1.5 x 19mm/¹⁄₁₆ x ¾in balsa
    wood strips
pair of compasses
emulsion (latex) paint: off-white,
    dark brown and brilliant white
medium and fine paintbrushes
exterior-grade varnish
drill with 3mm/⅛in bit
50 x 50mm/2 x 2in wooden post
screwdriver
75mm/3in screw, plus smaller
    screws

TYPICAL INHABITANTS
house and tree sparrows
tree swallows
bluebirds

1 Mark and cut out the basic house on to MDF or plywood following the template at the back. Assemble using glue and panel pins. Mark a sheet of veneer into 19 x 38mm/ ¾ x 1½in shingles and rub randomly with woodstain. Cut out the shingles with a scalpel or craft knife. Glue them in overlapping rows to the roof of the house.

2 Cut balsa wood strips to length to use as clapboarding. Glue in position. Set a pair of compasses to transfer the cutting angles or make paper templates to show the shapes to be cut. Paint the clapboarding with off-white emulsion and brown windows. Paint window frames and doors using a fine brush and white emulsion. Varnish.

3 Cut a base 200 x 125mm/8 x 5in from plywood. Drill pilot holes at each corner and in the centre. Fasten to the top of the post with a central 75mm/3in screw. Screw through the corners into the house.

TEMPLATES

The templates provided in the following pages will enable you to complete some of the more complex projects in this book. They should be used in conjunction with the instructions and cutting lists for the wood. Each template provides specific dimensions for the project. All the dimensions are listed in both metric and imperial measurements. You should decide which system you are going to use and then follow it, not mixing the two. You might like to make paper templates from these plans and arrange them on your wood before cutting. It's always a good idea to double-check your measurements before cutting.

Left: This hanging nest box with a small, round entrance hole will suit acrobatic species such as tits and wrens. It is best hung from a branch.

Above: *A nest box with a small entrance hole will suit tits, titmice, wrens and sparrows. A taller box would suit woodpeckers.*

Above: *Open-fronted nest boxes will attract robins, wrens, flycatchers and wagtails. Other species may use the box as a roost.*

Above: *Birdhouses such as this one look highly ornamental in the garden and can be finished according to personal taste.*

PALLADIAN BIRD TABLE, page 38

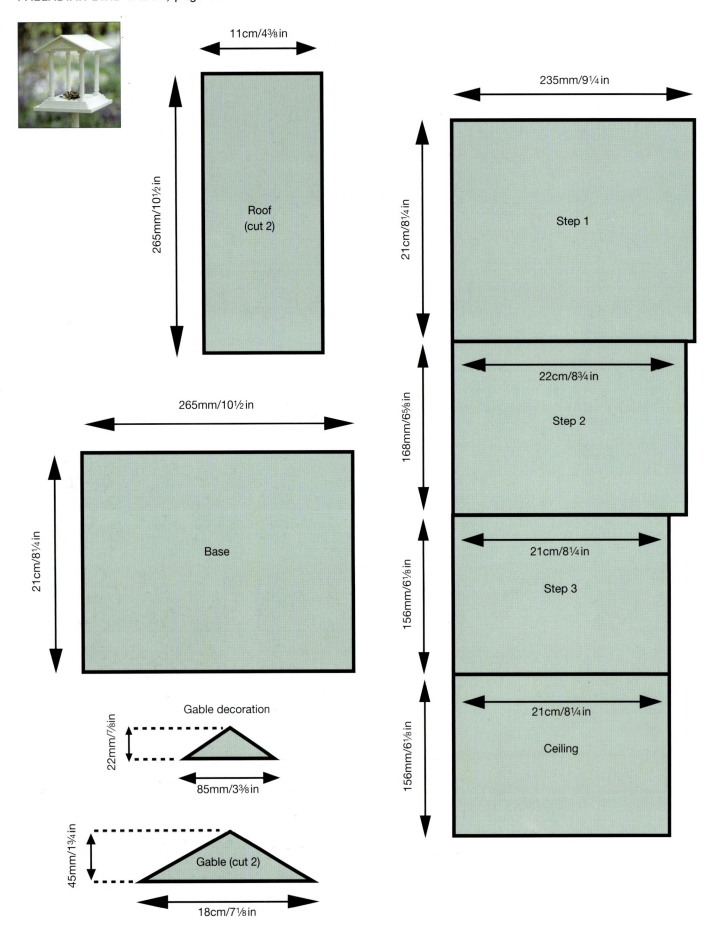

11cm/4⅜ in

265mm/10½ in

Roof
(cut 2)

235mm/9¼ in

21cm/8¼ in

Step 1

22cm/8¾ in

Step 2

168mm/6⅝ in

265mm/10½ in

Base

21cm/8¼ in

21cm/8¼ in

Step 3

156mm/6⅛ in

Gable decoration

22mm/⅞in

85mm/3⅜ in

21cm/8¼ in

Ceiling

156mm/6⅛ in

45mm/1¾in

Gable (cut 2)

18cm/7⅛ in

SEASIDE BIRD TABLE, page 40

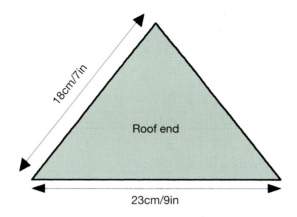

Roof end

18cm/7in

23cm/9in

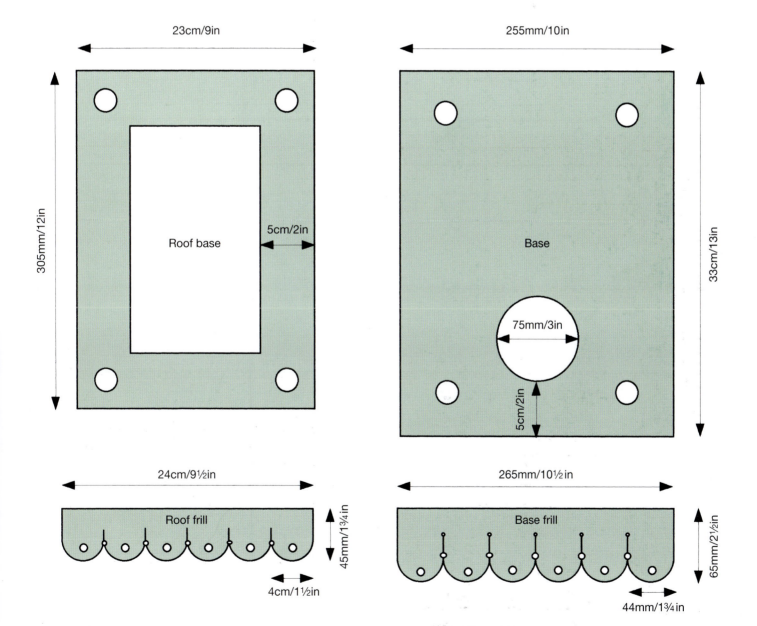

23cm/9in

Roof base

305mm/12in

5cm/2in

255mm/10in

Base

33cm/13in

75mm/3in

5cm/2in

24cm/9½in

Roof frill

45mm/1¾in

4cm/1½in

265mm/10½in

Base frill

65mm/2½in

44mm/1¾in

BAMBOO BIRD TABLE, page 42

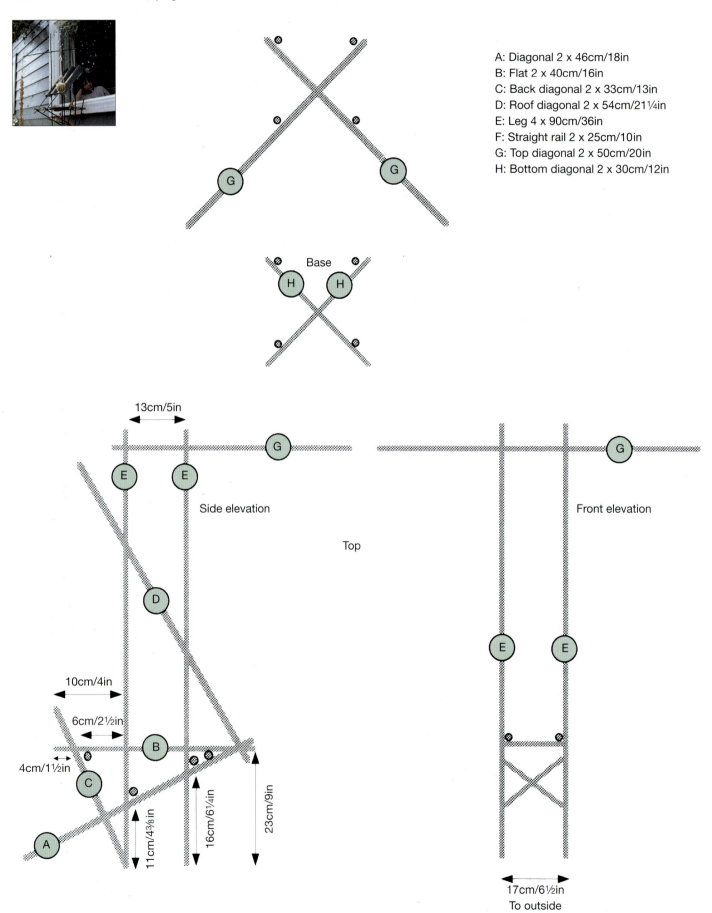

A: Diagonal 2 x 46cm/18in
B: Flat 2 x 40cm/16in
C: Back diagonal 2 x 33cm/13in
D: Roof diagonal 2 x 54cm/21¼in
E: Leg 4 x 90cm/36in
F: Straight rail 2 x 25cm/10in
G: Top diagonal 2 x 50cm/20in
H: Bottom diagonal 2 x 30cm/12in

Base

13cm/5in

Side elevation

Front elevation

Top

10cm/4in

6cm/2½in

4cm/1½in

11cm/4⅜in

16cm/6¼in

23cm/9in

17cm/6½in

To outside

ENCLOSED NEST BOX, page 58

OPEN-FRONTED NEST BOX, page 60

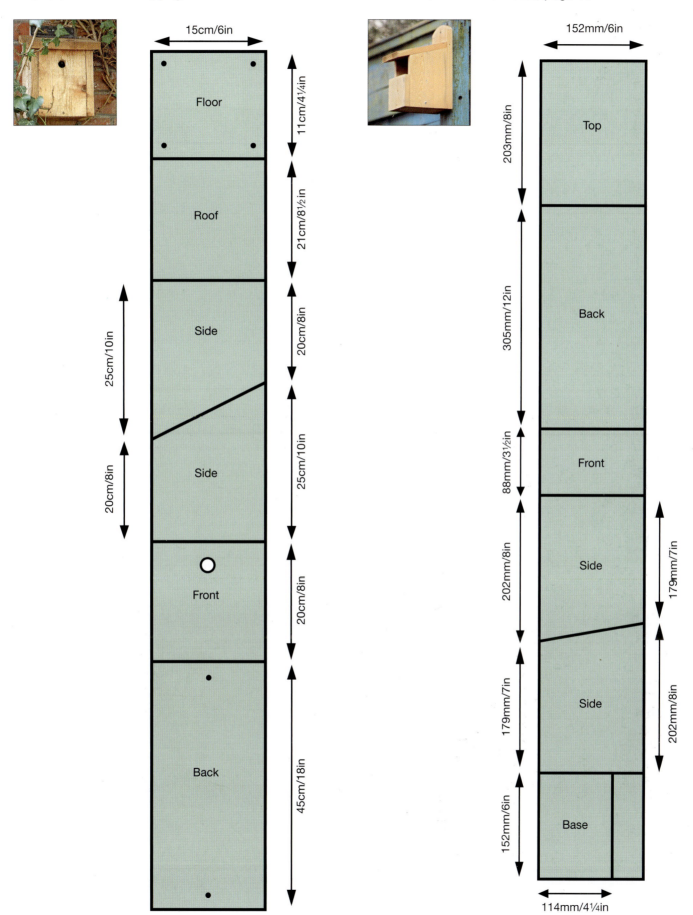

15cm/6in

Floor

Roof

Side

Side

Front

Back

11cm/4¼in

21cm/8½in

20cm/8in

25cm/10in

20cm/8in

45cm/18in

25cm/10in

20cm/8in

152mm/6in

Top

Back

Front

Side

Side

Base

203mm/8in

305mm/12in

88mm/3½in

202mm/8in

179mm/7in

152mm/6in

179mm/7in

202mm/8in

114mm/4¼in

LAVENDER HIDEAWAY, page 66

POST BOX, page 158

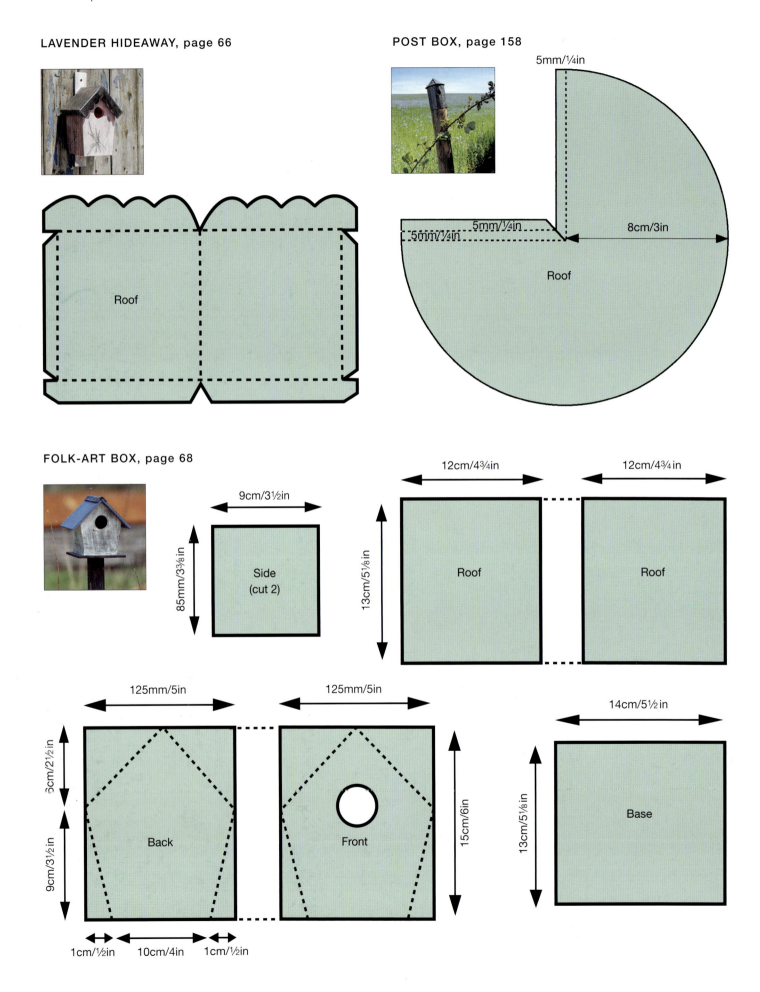

Roof

5mm/¼in

5mm/¼in

5mm/¼in

8cm/3in

Roof

FOLK-ART BOX, page 68

9cm/3½in

85mm/3⅜in

Side
(cut 2)

12cm/4¾in

12cm/4¾in

13cm/5⅛in

Roof

Roof

125mm/5in

125mm/5in

14cm/5½in

6cm/2½in

9cm/3½in

Back

15cm/6in

Front

13cm/5⅛in

Base

1cm/½in   10cm/4in   1cm/½in

ROCK-A-BYE BIRDIE BOX, page 70

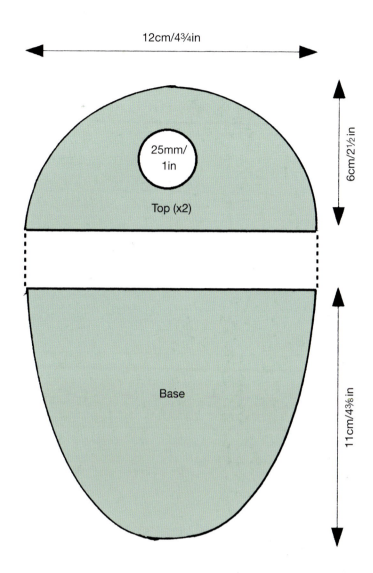

12cm/4¾in

25mm/
1in

Top (x2)

6cm/2½in

Base

11cm/4⅜in

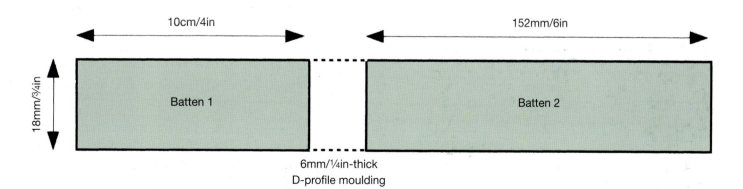

10cm/4in

152mm/6in

18mm/¾in

Batten 1

Batten 2

6mm/¼in-thick
D-profile moulding

SLATE-ROOFED COTTAGE, page 72

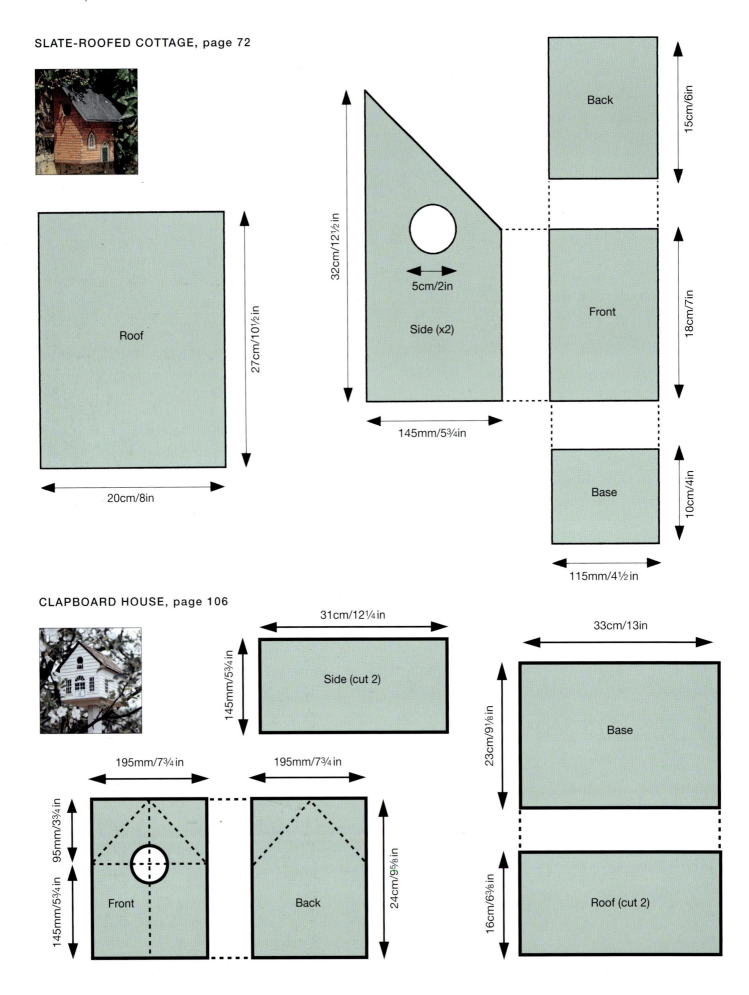

Roof

27cm/10½in

20cm/8in

32cm/12½in

Side (x2)

5cm/2in

145mm/5¾in

Back

15cm/6in

Front

18cm/7in

Base

10cm/4in

115mm/4½in

CLAPBOARD HOUSE, page 106

31cm/12¼in

Side (cut 2)

145mm/5¾in

195mm/7¾in

195mm/7¾in

95mm/3¾in

145mm/5¾in

Front

Back

24cm/9⅝in

33cm/13in

Base

23cm/9⅛in

Roof (cut 2)

16cm/6⅜in

RIDGE TILE RETREAT, page 74

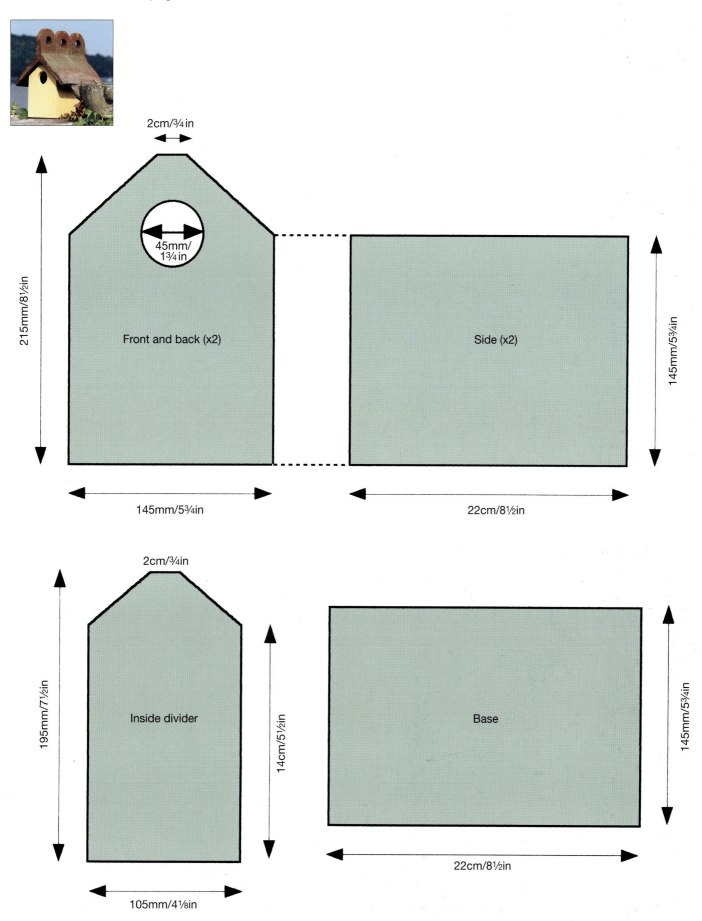

2cm/¾in

45mm/
1¾in

Front and back (x2)

Side (x2)

215mm/8½in

145mm/5¾in

145mm/5¾in

22cm/8½in

2cm/¾in

Inside divider

Base

195mm/7½in

14cm/5½in

145mm/5¾in

105mm/4⅛in

22cm/8½in

SWIFT NURSERY, page 76

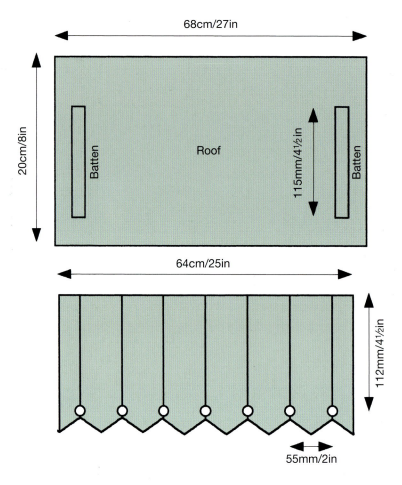

68cm/27in

20cm/8in

Batten

Roof

Batten

115mm/4½in

64cm/25in

112mm/4½in

55mm/2in

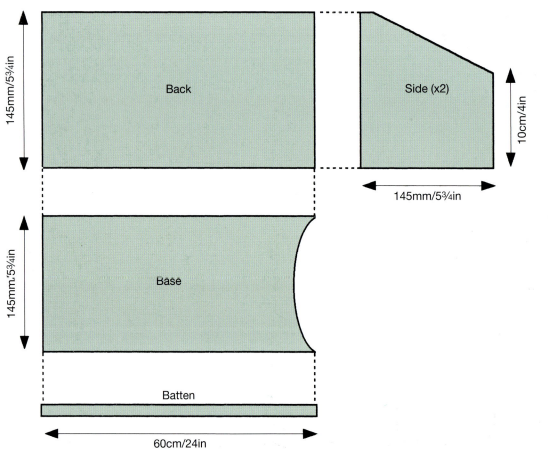

145mm/5¾in

Back

Side (x2)

10cm/4in

145mm/5¾in

145mm/5¾in

Base

Batten

60cm/24in

SEASIDE NEST BOX, page 82

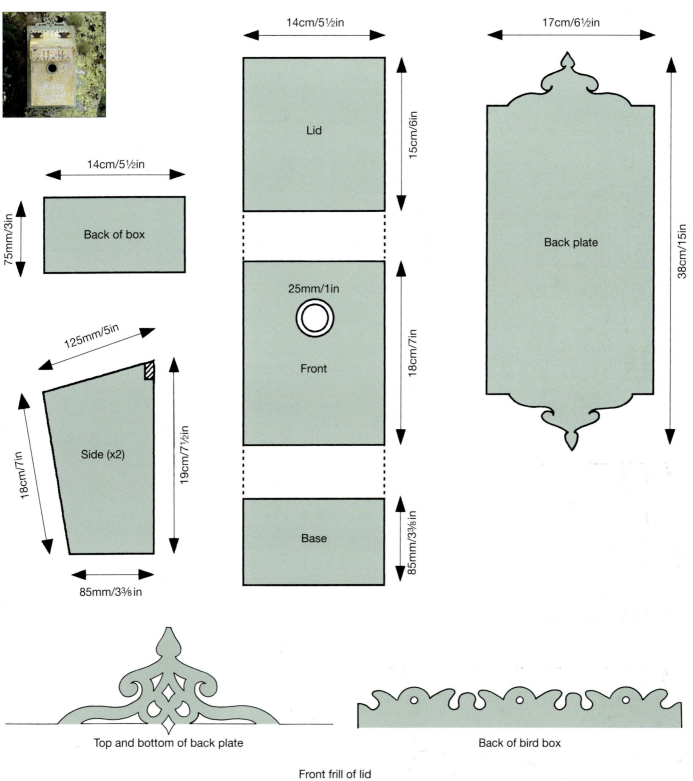

14cm/5½in

Back of box

75mm/3in

14cm/5½in

Lid

15cm/6in

17cm/6½in

Back plate

38cm/15in

125mm/5in

Side (x2)

18cm/7in

19cm/7½in

85mm/3⅜in

25mm/1in

Front

18cm/7in

Base

85mm/3⅜in

Top and bottom of back plate

Back of bird box

Front frill of lid

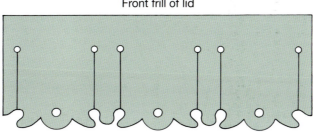

DUCK HOUSE, page 84

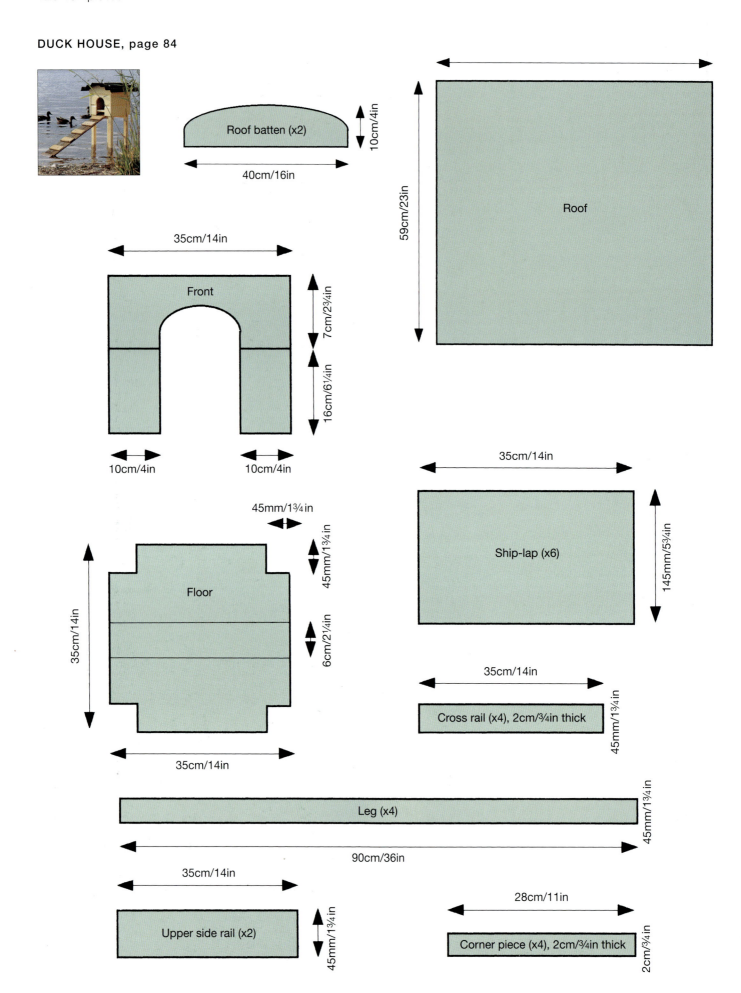

Roof batten (x2)

10cm/4in

40cm/16in

Roof

59/23in

35cm/14in

Front

7cm/2¾in

16cm/6¼in

10cm/4in

10cm/4in

45mm/1¾in

45mm/1¾in

Floor

6cm/2¼in

35cm/14in

35cm/14in

35cm/14in

Ship-lap (x6)

145mm/5¾in

35cm/14in

Cross rail (x4), 2cm/¾in thick

45mm/1¾in

Leg (x4)

45mm/1¾in

90cm/36in

35cm/14in

Upper side rail (x2)

45mm/1¾in

28cm/11in

Corner piece (x4), 2cm/¾in thick

2cm/¾in

RUSTIC CABIN, page 88

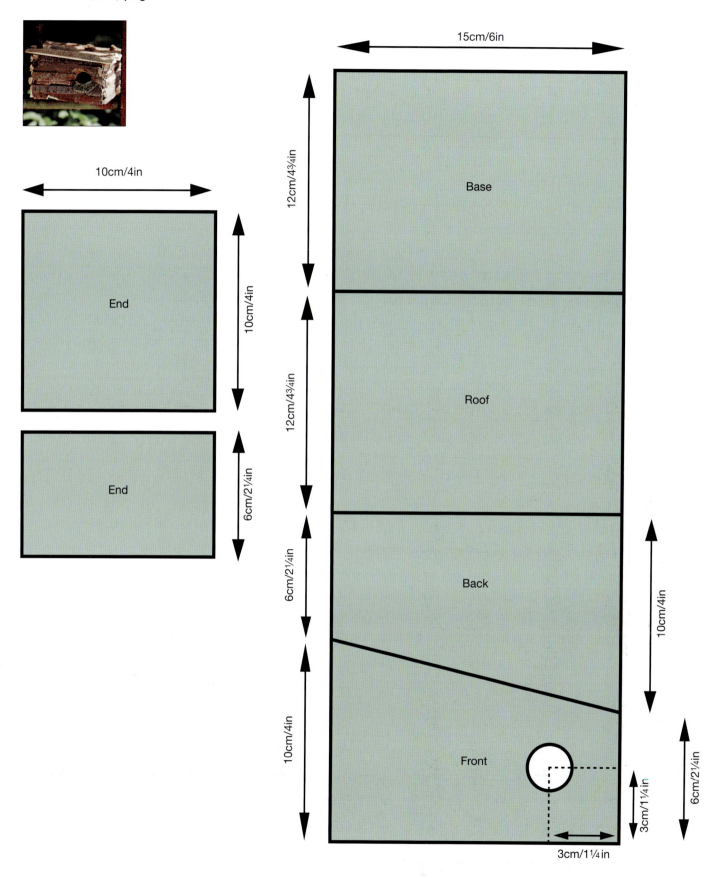

10cm/4in

End

10cm/4in

End

6cm/2¼in

15cm/6in

12cm/4¾in

Base

12cm/4¾in

Roof

6cm/2¼in

Back

10cm/4in

Front

10cm/4in

6cm/2¼in

3cm/1¼in

3cm/1¼in

THATCHED BIRDHOUSE, page 92

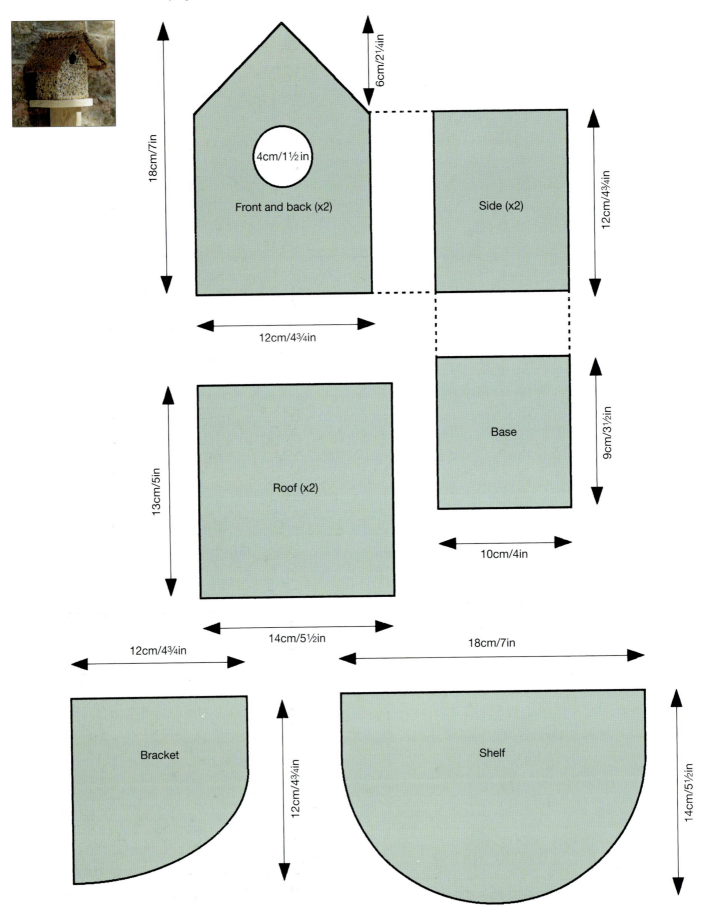

6cm/2¼in

18cm/7in

4cm/1½in

Front and back (x2)

Side (x2)

12cm/4¾in

12cm/4¾in

13cm/5in

Roof (x2)

Base

9cm/3½in

10cm/4in

14cm/5½in

12cm/4¾in

18cm/7in

Bracket

Shelf

12cm/4¾in

14cm/5½in

DOVECOTE, page 104

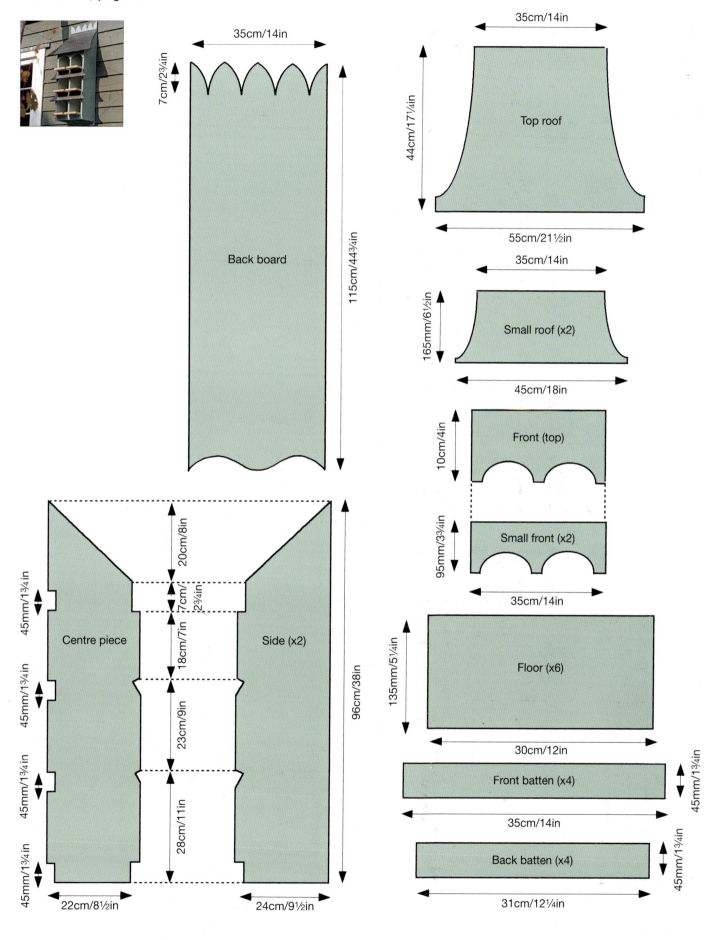

35cm/14in

7cm/2¾in

115cm/44¾in

Back board

35cm/14in

44cm/17¼in

Top roof

55cm/21½in

35cm/14in

165mm/6½in

Small roof (x2)

45cm/18in

10cm/4in

Front (top)

95mm/3¾in

Small front (x2)

35cm/14in

135mm/5¼in

Floor (x6)

30cm/12in

Front batten (x4)

45mm/1¾in

35cm/14in

Back batten (x4)

45mm/1¾in

31cm/12¼in

20cm/8in

7cm/2¾in

45mm/1¾in

Centre piece

Side (x2)

45mm/1¾in

18cm/7in

96cm/38in

45mm/1¾in

23cm/9in

45mm/1¾in

28cm/11in

45mm/1¾in

22cm/8½in

24cm/9½in

NEST BOX SIZES

The dimensions given here will enable you to modify basic nest box designs to suit a wide range of bird species. You may need to alter the dimensions slightly according to the thickness of your wood. Inner surfaces can be left rough, but you should drill a few small holes in the floor of the box for drainage.

ENCLOSED NEST BOXES

This style of nest box has a small, round entrance hole positioned high on the front face. Enclosed nest boxes are suitable for birds that usually nest in tree holes, such as wrens, tits, titmice, chickadees, sparrows, nuthatches, bluebirds, martins, finches, flycatchers and some swallows. Larger bird species, such as starlings, jackdaws, woodpeckers, flickers, owls, American kestrels and Carolina wood ducks, will nest in a larger box of this type, with a bigger entrance hole.

	Floor size	Depth of box	Height of entrance above floor	Diameter of entrance hole	Height above ground
EUROPE					
Wren	10 x 10cm/4 x 4in	15–20cm/6–8in	12cm/4½in	3cm/1¼in	Low in vegetation
Tits	15 x 12cm/6 x 4½in	20–25cm/8–10in	12cm/4½in	3cm/1¼in	2m/7ft
Sparrows	15 x 15cm/6 x 6in	20–25cm/8–10in	15cm/6in	3cm/1¼in	2–4m/7–14ft
Nuthatch	15 x 15cm/6 x 6in	20–25cm//8–10in	12cm/4½in	3cm/1¼in	3.6–6m/12–20ft
Starling	15 x 15cm/6 x 6in	40–45cm/16–18in	30cm/12in	5cm/2in	5m/16ft
Woodpeckers	15 x 15cm/6 x 6in	30–38cm/12–15in	40cm/16in	6cm/2½in	3–5m/10–16ft
Jackdaw	20 x 20cm/8 x 8in	30–38cm/12–15in	40cm/16in	15cm/6in	3–5m/10–16ft
Street pigeon	20 x 20cm/8 x 8in	30–38cm/12–15in	10cm/4in	10cm/4in	3–5m/10–16ft
NORTH AMERICA					
Chickadee	10 x 10cm/4 x 4in	8–10cm/20–25in	15–20cm/6–8in	3cm/1¼in	1.8–4.5m/6–15ft
Titmouse	10 x 10cm/4 x 4in	8–10cm/20–25in	15–20cm/6–8in	3cm/1¼in	1.8–4.5m/6–15ft
Nuthatch	10 x 10cm/4 x 4in	8–10cm/20–25in	15–20cm/6–8in	3cm/1¼in	3.6–6m/12–20ft
Wrens					
House wren	10 x 10cm/4 x 4in	15–20cm/6–8in	10–15cm/4–6in	2.5–3cm/1–1¼in	1.8–3m/6–10ft
Bewick's and					
Carolina wren	10 x 10cm/4 x 4in	15–20cm/6–8in	10–15cm/4–6in	3cm/1¼in	1.8–3m/6–10ft
Winter wren	10 x 10cm/4 x 4in	15–20cm/6–8in	10–15cm/4–6in	3cm/1¼in	1.8–3m/6–10ft
Bluebird	13 x 13cm/5 x 5in	20cm/8in	15cm/6in	4cm/1½in	1.5–3m/5–10ft
Violet-green swallow					
and tree swallow	13 x 13cm/5 x 5in	15–20cm/6–8in	2.5–13cm/1–5in	4cm/1½in	3–4.5m/10–15ft
Purple martin	15 x 15cm/6 x 6in	15cm/6in	2.5cm/1in	6cm/2½in	4.5–6m/15–20ft
House finch	15 x 15cm/6 x 6in	15cm/6in	10cm/4in	5cm/2in	2.4–3.6m/8–12ft
Crested flycatcher	15 x 15cm/6 x 6in	8–10cm/20–25in	15–20cm/6–8in	5cm/2in	2.4–6m/8–20ft
Starling	15 x 15cm/6 x 6in	40–46cm/16–18in	36–40cm/14–16in	5cm/2in	3–7.6m/10–25ft
Woodpeckers					
Downy	10 x 10cm/4 x 4in	8–10cm/20–25in	15–20cm/6–8in	3cm/1¼in	1.8–6m/6–20ft
Golden-fronted	15 x 15cm/6 x 6in	30–38cm/12–15in	22–30cm/9–12in	5cm/2in	3.6–6m/12–20ft
Red-headed	15 x 15cm/6 x 6in	30–38cm/12–15in	22–30cm/9–12in	5cm/2in	3.6–6m/12–20ft
Hairy	15 x 15cm/6 x 6in	30–38cm/12–15in	22–30cm/9–12in	4cm/1½in	3.6–6m/12–20ft
Flicker	18 x 18cm/7 x 7in	40–46cm/16–18in	36–40cm/14–16in	6cm/2½in	1.8–6m/6–20ft
Owls					
Saw-whet	15 x 15cm/6 x 6in	25–30cm/10–12in	20–25cm/8–10in	6cm/2½in	3.6–6m/12–20ft
Screech	20 x 20cm/8 x 8in	30–38cm/12–15in	22–30cm/9–12in	7.5cm/3in	3–9m/10–30ft
Barn	25 x 46cm/10 x 18in	38–46cm/15–18in	10cm/4in	15cm/6in	3.6–5.5m/12–18ft
American kestrel	20 x 20cm/8 x 8in	30–38cm/12–15in	22–30cm/9–12in	7.5cm/3in	3–9m/10–30ft
Carolina wood duck	25 x 46cm/10 x 18in	25–60cm/10–24in	30–40cm/12–16in	36cm/14in	3–6m/10–20ft

OPEN-FRONTED NEST BOXES

Not all birds like nest boxes with small entrance holes. The open-fronted types have a larger, rectangular entrance area at the front. This style of box is suitable for wrens and robins. A kestrel will nest in a larger box of this type.

	Floor size	Depth of box	Height to top of front	Positioning/comments
EUROPE				
Wren	10 x 10cm/4 x 4in	15cm/6in	10cm/4in	Low in dense vegetation
Robin	10 x 10cm/4 x 4in	15cm/6in	5cm/2in	1.5–5.5m/5–18ft above ground
Kestrel	30 x 50cm/12 x 20in	30cm/12in	15cm/6in	5m/16ft above ground

BIRD SHELVES

Nesting shelves – also known as roosting boxes – have an entirely open front, and may used for resting and sleeping as well as nesting. They are suitable for wagtails, spotted flycatchers, blackbirds, song sparrows, American robins, barn swallows and phoebes. Other species, such as blue jays and cardinals, may also roost or nest in this type of box.

	Floor size	Depth of box	Positioning/comments
EUROPE			
Pied wagtail	10 x 10cm/4 x 4in	10cm/4in	1.5–5.5m/5–18ft above ground
Spotted flycatcher	15 x 15cm/6 x 6in	10cm/4in	1.5–5.5m/5–18ft above ground
Blackbird	20 x 20cm/8 x 8in	20cm/8in	In dense vegetation
NORTH AMERICA			
Song sparrow	15 x 15cm/6 x 6in	15cm/6in	30–90cm/1–3ft above ground
American robin	15 x 15cm/6 x 6in	20cm/8in	1.8–4.5m/6–15ft above ground
Barn swallow	15 x 15cm/6 x 6in	15cm/6in	2.4–3.6m/8–12ft above ground
Phoebe	15 x 15cm/6 x 6in	15cm/6in	2.4–3.6m/8–12ft above ground

UNUSUAL NEST BOXES

Some species, such as members of the swift family, owls and ducks, require special types of nest boxes. Most are constructed of wood, but cup nests for swallows and house martins can be made of papier-mâché or a wood-chip mix.

	Description	Positioning/comments
EUROPE		
Swallow	Cup-shaped nest	On shed or stable
House martin	Cup-shaped nest	Fix under eaves of house or shed
Swift	Oblong box, 60 x 15 x 15cm/24 x 6 x 6in, with an entrance underneath	Place horizontally under eaves of house
Barn owl	Oblong box, 25 x 46 x 40cm/10 x 18 x 16in	4.5m/15ft above ground
Tawny owl	Oblong box, 76 x 26 x 22cm/30 x10½ x 9in	In a tree under a branch
Little owl	20 x 120 x 26cm/8in x 4ft x 10in, with a 10cm/4in hole 30cm/12in from the floor	In a tree
Mallard	35 x 35 x 33cm/14 x 14 x 13in	On an island or raft
NORTH AMERICA		
Mallard	35 x 35 x 33cm/14 x 14 x 13in	On an island or raft

Right: *A mallard house should be positioned on an island or raft to provide protection from predators. The ramp should have horizontal struts so that the ducks' feet do not slip when walking.*

USEFUL CONTACTS

UNITED KINGDOM
Organizations
British Birds Rarities Committee
http://www.bbrc.org.uk/

British Garden Birds
http://www.garden-birds.co.uk/

British Ornithologists' Club
http://www.boc-online.org/

British Ornithologists' Union
http://www.bou.org.uk/

British Trust for Ornithology (BTO)
http://www.bto.org.uk

BTO Garden Birdwatch
http://www.bto.org/gbw/

Fat Birder
http://www.fatbirder.com

Hawk Conservancy
http://www.hawk-conservancy.org/

Hawk and Owl Trust
http://www.hawkandowl.org/

Rare Breeding Birds Panel
http://www.rbbp.org.uk/

Royal Society for the Protection
of Birds (RSPB)
http://www.rspb.org.uk

Wildfowl & Wetlands Trust
http://www.wwt.org.uk

Advice on gardening for birds
Field Studies Council
www.field-studies-council.org

Flora locale
http://www.floralocale.org/

RSPB advice on gardening
http://www.rspb.org.uk/advice/gardening/

The Wildlife Trusts
www.wildlifetrusts.org

Bird box and food suppliers
CJ WildBird Foods Ltd
www.birdfood.co.uk

Food for Wild Birds
http://www.food4wildbirds.co.uk/

Garden Bird Supplies
http://www.gardenbird.com/

RSPB Shop: bird food
http://shopping.rspb.org.uk/c/Birdfood.htm

The Specialist Bird Food Company
www.wild-bird-food.co.uk

Vine House Farm Bird Foods
http://vinehousefarm.co.uk/

WWF Wildlife Shop
http://shop.wwf.org.uk/wildlife

NORTH AMERICA
Organizations
American Bird Conservancy
http://www.abcbirds.org/

American Birding Association
http://www.americanbirding.org/

American Ornithologists' Union
http://www.aou.org/

Audubon Society state contacts
http://www.audubon.org/chapter/
(Append state abbreviation at
the end of this URL, for example,
for Alaska, type:
http://www.audubon.org/chapter/ak)

Bird Studies Canada
http://www.bsc-eoc.org/

Bird Watcher's Digest magazine
http://www.birdwatchersdigest.com

Birding in Canada
http://www.web-nat.com/bic/

Birdnet.com
http://www.nmnh.si.edu/BIRDNET/

Birdzilla.com
http://www.birdzilla.com/

Canadian Nature Federation
http://www.cnf.ca/

Canadian Peregrine Foundation
http://www.peregrine-foundation.ca/

Canadian Wildlife Service
http://www.cws-scf.ec.gc.ca

Cooper Ornithological Association
http://www.cooper.org/

Cornell Lab of Ornithology
http://birds.cornell.edu

National Audubon Society
http://www.audubon.org/

National Parks, Forests, Wilderness Areas
http://gorp.away.com/gorp/resource/

National Wildlife Federation
http://www.nwf.org/

North American Bird Sounds
http://www.naturesongs.com/birds.html

North American Rare Bird Alert
http://www.narba.org/

Ornithological Societies of North America
http://www.osnabirds.org/

Sierra Club
http://www.sierraclub.org/

US Fish & Wildlife Service
http://www.fws.gov/

Advice on gardening for birds
Birds-n-garden
http://www.birds-n-garden.com/
birdgarden.html

Cornell Lab of Ornithology
http://www.birds.cornell.edu/AllAboutBirds/
attracting/landscaping/

Council on the Environment of New York City
http://www.cenyc.org/files/citylot/
Birds_in_Urban_Gardens.pdf

National Wildlife Federation
http://www.nwf.org/backyard/

NSiS: Florida Native Plants
http://www.nsis.org/garden/
garden-native-birds.html

Bird box and food suppliers
The Backyard Bird Company
http://www.backyardbird.com/

The Bird Feeders Society
http://www.thebirdfeederssociety.com/

Birds-n-garden
http://www.birds-n-garden.com/

Duncraft
http://www.duncraft.com/

Krismer's Plant Farm bird feed chart
http://www.krismers.com/
Bird_Feeding_Chart.pdf

National Bird-Feeding Society
http://www.birdfeeding.org/

Wild Bird Habitat Store
http://www.wildbirdhabitatstore.com/

CENTRAL AND SOUTH AMERICA
Caribbean Species Listings
http://camacdonald.com/birding/
Comparisons-Caribbean.htm

Central American Species Listings
http://camacdonald.com/birding/
Comparisons-CentralAm.htm

Neotropical Bird Club
http://www.neotropicalbirdclub.org

South American Species Listings
http://camacdonald.com/birding/
Comparisons-SouthAmerica.htm

AUSTRALIA AND NEW ZEALAND
Birds Australia
http://www.birdsaustralia.com.au

Bird Observers Club of Australia
http://www.birdobservers.org.au

New Zealand Birds and Birding
http://www.nzbirds.com/

Ornithological Society of
New Zealand
http://www.osnz.org.nz/

Royal Forest and Bird Protection Society
of New Zealand
www.forestandbird.org.nz

ASIA
Oriental Bird Club
http://www.orientalbirdclub.org

EUROPE/MIDDLE EAST
European Ornithologists' Union
http://www.eou.at

Ornithological Society of the
Middle East
http://www.osme.org/

AFRICA
African Bird Club
http://www.africanbirdclub.org

African Bird Club: South Africa
http://www.africanbirdclub.org/countries/
SouthAfrica/conservation.html

Birdlife South Africa
http://www.birdlife.org.za/

West African Ornithological Society
http://malimbus.free.fr/

INTERNATIONAL ORGANIZATIONS
BirdLife International
http://www.birdlife.org/

European Ornithologists' Union
http://www.eou.at

International Ornithological Committee
http://www.i-o-c.org/IOComm/

Neotropical Bird Club
http://www.neotropicalbirdclub.org/

Pacific Seabird Group
http://www.pacificseabirdgroup.org/

Rare Birds of the World
http://www.geocities.com/RainForest/
Vines/2408/critical.html

Surfbirds.com
http://www.surfbirds.com/

Working Group on International Waderbird
and Wetland Research
http://home.wanadoo.nl/rene.t.vos/wiwo/
wiwo1.htm

INDEX

ACKNOWLEDGEMENTS

The publisher would like to thank the following for allowing their photographs to be reproduced in the book (l = left, r = right, t = top, m = middle, b = bottom):

Felicity Forster: 11tl, 25l, 57l, 57r.

iStockphoto: 6t, 7, 9r, 10, 11tr, 13tl, 16tr, 16tr, 16b, 17b, 18t, 18b, 19tr, 26b, 30tl, 32tl, 34t, 38tl, 40tl, 42tl, 44tl, 48tl, 54bl, 57m, 60tl, 62tl, 66bl, 70tl, 72tl, 74br, 78tl, 80tl, 82tl, 84t, 84m, 88b, 90tl, 92tl, 94tl, 96tl, 98bl, 100tl, 102tl, 104tl, 106tl, 126t, 126b, 127t, 127b.

NHPA/Photoshot: 76tl (Alan Barnes).